THE REFERENCE SHELF   VOLUME 46 NUMBER 5

THE COMMON MARKET

EDITED BY
NANCY L. HOEPLI

Senior Editor, Foreign Policy Association

Portland Public Library

THE H. W. WILSON COMPANY
NEW YORK   1975

THE REFERENCE SHELF

The books in this series contain reprints of articles, excerpts from books, and addresses on current issues and social trends in the United States and other countries. There are six separately bound numbers in each volume, all of which are generally published in the same calendar year. One number is a collection of recent speeches; each of the others is devoted to a single subject and gives background information and discussion from various points of view, concluding with a comprehensive bibliography. Books in the series may be purchased individually or on subscription.

Library of Congress Cataloging in Publication Data

Hoepli, Nancy L   comp.
   The Common Market.

   (The Reference shelf ; v. 46, no. 5)
   Bibliography: p.
   SUMMARY: A compilation of reprinted articles discus-
sing the history of the Common Market, its strengths
and weaknesses, its relations with the United States,
and its future.
   1.   European Economic Community. [1.   European
Economic Community. 2.   Europe--Economic integration]
I.   Title. II.   Series.
HC241.2.H56   341.24'2   74-31185
ISBN 0-8242-0525-1

PREFACE

In an age of growing interdependence among nations, when there is an urgent need to develop new institutions to accommodate that interdependence, Europe's experiment known as the Common Market (formally called the European Economic Community) is being closely watched. The Common Market's nine European members today constitute the world's largest single trading bloc. By 1980, if they attain their goals, they will form a single political, social, economic, and monetary union, the European Community.

The Common Market was founded in 1958. In 1968, a year and a half ahead of schedule, it completed the formation of a customs union. Industrial goods and most farm produce moved freely among the six founding members—Belgium, France, Italy, West Germany, the Netherlands, and Luxembourg—and goods imported from nonmember countries were subject to a common tariff. Five years later, three new members—Britain, Denmark, and Ireland—joined the community, a testament to the Common Market's past success and promising future.

The year 1973 opened with celebrations over the Common Market's enlargement; it ended in crisis. Not since the decline of the Soviet menace had Western Europe's economic strength and stability been more severely tested. The crisis is not over. Rampant inflation, payments deficits, monetary instability, and even the danger of insolvency darken the horizon.

The coming years will be critical ones for the Common Market—and for the international economic order. Either the nine (assuming Britain and Denmark do not withdraw) will achieve greater integration and cooperation, or individual members will succumb to nationalistic tendencies, putting self-interest above the common interest. Either the

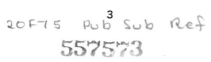

community will evolve into a formidable political power or it will dissolve into a loose grouping of nine struggling states wedged between two colossi.

The future of the Common Market today is in doubt. If it succeeds, it will serve as an example of how to institutionalize interdependence. If it fails, not only the European, but the international, economic system will suffer.

The editor wishes to thank the publishers and organizations that have courteously granted permission for the reprinting of their materials in this book. She is deeply indebted to Molly Bower Kux for her counsel and for her help in compiling the bibliography.

NANCY L. HOEPLI

November 1974

CONTENTS

III. UNFINISHED BUSINESS

IV. THE AMERICAN CONNECTION

V. LOOKING AHEAD TO 1980

GLOSSARY

CAP: Abbreviation for the Common Market's Common Agricultural Policy, which establishes a system of supports and import controls. It now covers over 90 percent of the Common Market's agricultural production.

COMMON MARKET: Popular name for the European Economic Community. See EC below.

COMMUNITY OF NINE: The six founding members and three new members—the United Kingdom, Ireland, and Denmark. See EC below.

COMMUNITY OF SIX: European Communities. See EC below.

CUSTOMS UNION: A group of countries that eliminates tariffs on internal trade and adopts a common tariff on imports from the rest of the world.

EC: European Community or European Communities. The collective name for the European Coal and Steel Community, the European Economic Community, and the European Atomic Energy Community. Founding members were Belgium, France, Italy, West Germany, the Netherlands, and Luxembourg. The United Kingdom, Ireland, and Denmark joined on January 1, 1973.

ECSC: European Coal and Steel Community.

EEC: European Economic Community.

EFTA: European Free Trade Association, established in 1960. Members are Norway, Sweden, Switzerland, Austria, Portugal, and Iceland; Finland is an associate member. Denmark and the United Kingdom are former members.

EMU: The proposed Economic and Monetary Union.

FREE TRADE AREA: A group of countries that eliminates tariffs on internal trade but does not adopt a common tariff on imports from the rest of the world.

VARIABLE LEVY: Applied by the Common Market to certain agricultural imports to raise prices to the level of the market's guaranteed minimum price for that product.

VAT: Value Added Tax. An indirect tax which has the effect of a retail sales tax. The tax is collected on the value added to a product at each stage of production before the product reaches the consumer.

I. IN THE BEGINNING

EDITOR'S INTRODUCTION

The Common Market owes its existence to men of vision who dreamed of a united Europe. Among those men was France's Jean Monnet. As far back as World War I, Monnet tried to bridge the frontiers separating Europeans, as Boyd France reveals in the first article in this section. The movement for economic and political union in Western Europe gained new urgency in the wake of World War II. The steps that led to the formation of the three European communities—the European Atomic Energy Community, the European Coal and Steel Community, and the European Economic Community—are recorded in the second selection. A description of how the communities' institutions work—at least in principle—follows. The New York *Times'* Nan Robertson draws a candid portrait, warts and all, of one of these institutions, the European Parliament. And the *Economist* describes the men who keep the institutions' machinery running, the "Eurocrats" of Brussels.

On January 1, 1973, fifteen years after the Common Market was founded, it celebrated a major milestone: the accession of three new members—Britain, Denmark, and Ireland. *Senior Scholastic* explores the meaning of enlargement for the member states, for Eastern Europe, and for the United States. In the final selection, Clyde H. Farnsworth of the New York *Times* takes a close look at the Common Market at the time of its enlargement and finds that progress toward European unification is not only steady, but probably irreversible.

THE COMMON MARKET:
A PROCESS, NOT A PRODUCT [1]

Many Europeans have contributed to the building of Europe but above all it is the work of Jean Monnet, wine merchant, economic planner, and statesman. His efforts to persuade European governments to reach beyond narrow considerations to grasp their common interest began in World War I. This international businessman saw Britain and France each buying and shipping supplies to their individual armies engaged in a common war. His resource-saving idea was the formation of a joint Franco-British Supply Commission for which he fought and on which he served. He inspired and headed a similar organization in World War II.

On the eve of the fall of France, in June 1940, Monnet proposed to British Prime Minister Winston S. Churchill and French President Charles de Gaulle the proclamation of a Franco-British political union and joint citizenship. Churchill agreed and made the offer to France public. Monnet borrowed a British plane and flew to Bordeaux, to which the French government had retreated before the advancing German army. He failed to persuade the French cabinet to return with him to London to proclaim the union. Undaunted, he resumed his crusade to unite Europe after the war.

His was the seminal inspiration for the Schuman Plan to pool European coal and steel industries under a supranational High Authority. Later Monnet saw the need and the opportunity for creating a supranational European Defense Community to counter the Soviet threat to Europe. After the French National Assembly rejected that initiative, it was Monnet who rallied the governments of France, Ger-

[1] From *A Short Chronicle of United States-European Community Relations*, pamphlet by Boyd France, international affairs correspondent in Washington for McGraw-Hill Publications. European Community Information Service. 2100 M Street, N.W. Washington, D.C. 20037. '73. p 3-4.

many, Italy, Belgium, the Netherlands, and Luxembourg to take a bold stride towards European union by forging the European Economic Community (Common Market [or EEC]) and by pooling their peaceful nuclear industries within the European Atomic Energy Community (Euratom).

Monnet labored patiently from the outset to bring Britain into the European movement. He was frustrated, first by British and later by French nationalistic misgivings. Today, his faith that Britain would one day join Europe has been vindicated.

In October 1955, Monnet, concerned that the long-term end of European political unity should not be lost through preoccupation with the economic means, formed the Action Committee for the United States of Europe. This pressure group of influential European political, labor, and business leaders was the first of its kind in Europe. It continues to serve as the community nations' "conscience," reminding them of their larger European objectives.

Although "Mr. Europe," as Monnet is called affectionately, has dedicated his life to the creation of a strong and united Europe, he has insisted that this Europe must be a partner, and not a rival, of the United States. Monnet has been intimately involved with the United States for most of his life, first as a merchant, later, after the defeat of France, as a member of the British Supply Council. He played a key role in fashioning President Franklin D. Roosevelt's aircraft production program. He coined the slogan "the arsenal of democracy" and produced the concept of "lend-lease."

Monnet has been the friend and counselor of two generations of American statesmen, from Cordell Hull to Henry A. Kissinger. He has thought of the United States not only as Europe's friend and ally but also as its model. On the tenth anniversary of the signing of the Rome treaties creating the European Economic Community and the European Atomic Energy Community (Euratom), Monnet said:

Americans should understand better than anyone the benefits for Europe and the world of the peaceful revolution that is taking place in Europe, for America too is a common market whose states apply common laws through their common federal institutions.

The Common Market is a process, not a product. Europe is on the way to achieving economic unity, but we must have no doubt that in due course it will move towards unity in foreign policy and defense. What is gradually emerging is a great new entity, the United States of Europe.

OUT OF THE ASHES [2]

For centuries idealists have advocated the peaceful union of Europe. The postwar movement towards economic and political unity in Western Europe arose out of the suffering and destruction of World War II and the resulting determination to prevent another conflict in Europe.

The Second World War had brought defeat and occupation, at one time or another, to all six community countries. The limitations of national sovereignty in economic and political affairs were vividly brought home to many of their citizens.

Britain, on the other hand, emerged from the war undefeated and unoccupied, and her national institutions were regarded as vindicated and strengthened. There was little popular pressure for European unity. Elsewhere in Western and Northern Europe, Sweden, Switzerland and Ireland had remained neutral during the war, and were determined to maintain their neutrality. Denmark and Norway, though both had been occupied during the war, had strong links with Britain and Sweden. None of these countries took part in establishing the communities in the 1950s.

Western European countries, threatened by the expansionist policies of Soviet Russia, especially after the takeover of Poland and Hungary and the 1948 coup d'état in Czecho-

[2] From *European Community: The Facts,* pamphlet published by the Commission of the European Communities. European Community Information Service. 2100 M Street, N.W. Washington, D.C. 20037. '72. p 4.

slovakia, felt a common need to resist this pressure. Countries which for centuries had played a major role in world affairs found, when acting individually, that they were no longer able to influence world events. The leaders of the six countries were prepared to seek a solution in common.

Coal and Steel

The first of the three communities, the European Coal and Steel Community [ECSC], was successfully launched as a pilot plan for future integration in Europe on May 9, 1950. Inspired by the ideas of Jean Monnet, the man responsible for the French national economic plan, Robert Schuman, foreign minister of France, on that day publicly appealed to the nations of Europe, and to Germany in particular, to pool their coal and steel under a common authority. Five nations—Belgium, Germany, Italy, Luxembourg and the Netherlands—responded favorably to the French proposal. In 1951 the six countries signed the Paris Treaty.

Although similar efforts in the 1950s to set up European defense and political communities failed, the coal and steel community succeeded, and encouraged the six to try to extend the formula to the whole field of economic activity. At a conference held in June 1955 in Messina, Italy, the six of the coal and steel community produced a plan for two new communities, the European Economic Community (or the Common Market) and the European Atomic Energy Community (Euratom).

The six countries had seen in the coal and steel sector the advantages of a vast single market where goods could move as freely between Rome and Amsterdam as between London and Glasgow.

The creation of one multinational unit with 180 million people, instead of 50 million as in France or Germany, was expected to promote greater wealth and economic stability than a single nation of 50 million or fewer inhabitants.

Finally, it was hoped that economic integration would help lead to the long-term goal of political unity.

Common Market

Experience gained in the ECSC helped in the establishment in 1958 of the European Economic Community and Euratom. The successful ECSC institutions—an independent executive (the High Authority), Council, Parliamentary Assembly, and Court—provided a blueprint for the introduction of such institutions in the wider European Economic Community. While under the ECSC treaty the balance of decision making lies with the executive (previously the High Authority and now the single Commission), under the EEC treaty it rests with the Council of Ministers.

The Common Market was to be created over a transition period of twelve years, beginning on January 1, 1958. Some of the objectives were achieved ahead of schedule. By July 1, 1968, one and a half years ahead of the original target date, there was free trade within the community both in industrial goods and in most farm produce. The six had eliminated intracommunity tariffs, and established a common tariff on goods imported from nonmember countries. When the transition period ended on schedule on December 31, 1969, most of the tasks had been accomplished. Others, like the common transport and energy policies, were behind schedule. In addition to its specific economic accomplishments, the community had brought about a new form of relationship between countries.

At The Hague in December 1969 the heads of state of the six agreed to advance from a customs union to full economic and monetary union. They also agreed to open membership negotiations with the UK, Ireland, Denmark and Norway. [Norwegian voters subsequently rejected membership.—Ed.]

HOW THE COMMUNITY WORKS [3]

The enlargement of the European communities on January 1, 1973, to include the United Kingdom, Ireland and Denmark, did not affect the basic structure and competence of the communities' four institutions—the European Parliament, the Council of Ministers, the Commission and the Court of Justice—although their composition was altered.

Until July 1967 the three communities—the European Coal and Steel Community (set up in 1952), the European Economic Community (1958) and the European Atomic Energy Community (1958)—had separate executive Commissions . . . and Councils of Ministers, while the parliament and court had been competent for all three communities since 1958. Since 1967 there has been a single Commission and a single council which exercise all the powers and responsibilities formerly vested in their respective predecessors, in the same way and in accordance with the same rules, as laid down in the three community treaties.

The merger of the institutions was no more than a first step towards the setting up of a single European Community, governed by a single treaty which will replace the Paris Treaty (establishing the ECSC) and the Rome treaties (establishing the Common Market and Euratom).

The Four Institutions

With the enlargement of the community the number of seats in the European Parliament was increased from 142 to 198. The total comprises 36 for each of the larger countries (France, Germany, Italy and the United Kingdom), 14 each for Belgium and the Netherlands, 10 each for Ireland and Denmark, and 6 for Luxembourg. Its members are appointed by the nine national parliaments from among their own members.

[3] From *How the European Community's Institutions Work,* pamphlet by Emile Noël, secretary general of the Commission of the European Communities. (Community Topics 39) European Community Information Office. 2100 M Street, N.W. Washington, D.C. 20037. '73. p 2-3, 7-10.

The council is made up of representatives of the governments of the nine member states. Each government normally sends one of its ministers, though on occasions more than one minister may be present. Its membership thus varies according to the matter up for consideration: The foreign minister is regarded in a sense as his country's "main" representative on the council, but council meetings are often attended by the ministers of agriculture, transport, finance, industry and so on, usually on their own, sometimes alongside the foreign minister.

The chairmanship of the council rotates between the member governments at six-monthly intervals in the following order: Belgium, Denmark, Germany, France, Ireland, Italy, Luxembourg, Netherlands, United Kingdom. (The rota began in the first half of 1973 with Belgium.)

When decisions are taken in the council by majority vote the four larger countries have 10 votes each, Belgium and the Netherlands 5 each, Ireland and Denmark 3 each and Luxembourg 2. This makes a total of 58 votes. For a proposal to be passed by a qualified majority vote 41 votes in favor are needed where the treaties require acts of the council to be adopted on a proposal from the Commission. In other circumstances, 41 votes in favor, cast by at least 6 member states, are required. . . .

The Commission consists of thirteen members, appointed by agreement between the member governments. Throughout their tenure of office the members must act in full independence both of the governments and of the council. The council cannot remove any member from office; only the parliament can if it wishes, by passing a vote of censure, compel the Commission to resign as a body.

The Court of Justice consists of nine judges appointed for terms of six years by the common consent of the governments, who see to it that the action taken to implement the treaties is in accordance with the rule of law. They are assisted in reaching their decisions by four advocates general. . . .

In the three communities (ECSC, EEC, Euratom), the Court of Justice, as well as affording the member states and individuals the assurance of full compliance with the treaty and the enactments implementing it, plays a notable part in ensuring uniform interpretation and enforcement of community law.

Financing the Community

On the Commission's proposal and following the political guidelines agreed upon at The Hague Conference of Heads of States and Governments (December 1969), the Council of Ministers gave their approval in 1970 for a system to be set up granting the community certain financial resources of its own. Owing to its unusual character, the six parliaments of the member states had to approve this decision, in accordance with the EEC treaty, before its entry into force on January 1, 1971.

This new system is being introduced gradually between 1971 and the end of 1977. During a first period (1971 to the end of 1974), only a part of community expenditure will be covered by revenue of its own. This revenue will consist of levies on imported agricultural products, which since the beginning of 1971 without exception have formed part of the community's own resources, and of an increasing proportion of customs duties. The remaining amount of revenue necessary for a balanced budget is still met by national contributions calculated on the basis of an overall scale taking account of each country's Gross National Product (GNP). . . .

The three new member countries are adopting the community's financing system by stages. Over the period 1973-77 inclusive they will gradually increase the proportion of the community's annual budget which they provide, until in 1977 it reaches 19.32 percent for the United Kingdom, 0.61 percent for Ireland and 2.46 percent for Denmark. In the years 1978 and 1979 the new countries' contribution will also be subject to limits, but in 1980 and after the full community system will operate for these countries, as it will have done from 1978 onwards for the six original community members.

The Commission–Council Dialogue

The European treaties assign the Commission a wide range of duties which may be roughly grouped as follows. The Commission is the guardian of the treaties; it is the executive arm of the communities; and it is the initiator of community policy and exponent of the community interest to the council. . . .

Under the Rome treaties, any measure of general application or a certain level of importance has to be enacted by the Council of Ministers, but except in a very few cases the council can only proceed upon proposal by the Commission. The Commission has thus a permanent duty to initiate action. If it submits no proposals, the council is paralyzed and the forward march of the community comes to a halt—in agriculture, in transport, in commercial policy, in harmonization of laws, or whatever the field concerned may be.

As an indication of the volume of the Commission's and council's work under the three treaties, it may be mentioned that in 1972 the Commission laid before the council 467 proposals and 234 memoranda and other documents of various kinds.

During 1972 the council, in addition to dealing with purely procedural matters and with budgets and financial regulations, adopted 264 regulations, 28 directives, and 44 decisions. . . .

A proposal having been lodged, a dialogue begins between the ministers of the council, putting their national points of view, and the Commission, in its capacity as the European body upholding the interest of the community as a whole and seeking European solutions to common problems.

There might seem to be some risk of the dialogue being

distorted by the Commission's being less strongly placed than the governments with the weight of their sovereign authority behind them. However, the Rome treaties contrive rather ingeniously to ensure that the two are evenly matched.

In the Commission's favor there is, for a start, the fact that it draws up the proposal the council is to deliberate—and only on the basis of that proposal can the council deliberate at all. . . .

Now this dialogue has a momentum of its own. The application of the majority rule, as fairly substantial EEC experience has shown, does not mean that a state is liable to find itself outvoted at the drop of a hat. The Commission in drawing up its proposal will have been careful to take into account the often widely-varying interests of the individual states and seek to establish where the general interest lies. As is usual in a club of so few members, both the members of the council and the Commission like to be in agreement if they can. Hence, if faced with the prospect of being outvoted, a minister may feel it best to abandon an extreme or isolated position, while for the sake of good relations the Commission, and those of the council who are in favor of its proposal, may make the necessary efforts to help secure a *rapprochement*. The result—a trifle paradoxical, but amply confirmed in practice—is that the majority rule makes for much easier and quicker arrival at unanimity. In this delicate interplay of forces, the Commission is always in a position to sway the outcome.

The Commission is thus centrally placed in the council, able regularly to act as "honest broker" among the governments, and to apply the prompting and pressure required to evolve formulas acceptable all round.

The implications for policy making are more important still. The Commission's proposals embody a policy prepared by it on the basis purely of the interest of the community as a whole. The fact that the Commission is there to stay throughout its term of office ensures the continuity of that policy, and the council can pronounce only on the Commission's proposed enactments for putting the policy into effect. There is therefore no danger that the council might adopt conflicting proposals on different issues in consequence of shifting majorities arising out of alliances of interests or contests of influence among governments.

Nor can it happen that a majority of the council, unbacked by the Commission, can impose on a recalcitrant state a measure gravely deleterious to that state's essential interests. If the Commission does its job properly, it can be no party to such a proceeding. Its role thus affords an important safeguard, more especially to the smaller member states, and they in particular have always set great store by this. . . .

The European Parliament

For the dialogue between Commission and council to be a genuine one, it is necessary that the Commission should be genuinely independent. To this end, the treaties make it answerable to the European Parliament alone.

The parliament is so constituted as to be in fact truly community in character, fully integrated. There are no national sections; there are only European-level political groups. The parliament keeps constant watch on the Commission's doings, making sure that it faithfully represents the community interest, ready at any time to call it to order if it gives the impression of yielding to blandishments from the governments or from a particular government. In addition, the parliament has to be expressly consulted on the Commission's more important proposals under the Rome treaties before these go to the council.

The parliament's various committees play a notable part in this connection. The house itself normally meets in ordinary session seven or eight times a year, for a week at a time (plus, on occasion, a number of extraordinary sessions of two days). Between sessions, each of the parliamentary committees meets at least once, and frequently several times, and the appropriate member of the Commission appears before it to give an account of the decisions taken by the Commission, the decisions referred to the council, and the position adopted by the Commission vis-à-vis the council.

The committees thus follow developments in detail, and as they meet *in camera* they can be told a great deal, including even confidential matter. Their work has done much to increase the parliament's influence in the day-to-day handling of affairs. . . .

By means of oral questions put in plenary session of the house (which may or may not be followed by a debate), the parliament is enabled to keep a careful eye on developments in European policy, both generally and with respect to particular sectors, and to comment directly at the time, sidestepping the sometimes rather unwieldy procedure of statements by the Commission, sending to committee, and reports to the full house. The parliament has in the last few years been making more and more use of this very flexible and effective device, putting oral questions both to the Commission and to the council. . . .

Increased Powers

At the same time as the council decided to grant the community a system of financial resources of its own, the member states signed a protocol on April 22, 1970, to alter the community treaties in order to increase the parliament's budgetary powers. This increase of powers applies to the "free" part of the budget, i.e., basically, the part which deals with the functioning of the community's institutions. . . .

The sums in question may seem limited in comparison with the total amount of the budget (they are often reckoned to amount to about 5 percent), but the power to control them assumes great political importance, because they determine the means whereby the community's institutions may work and carry out inquiries and studies, i.e. everything which guarantees their independent functioning. Not only will the parliament be able to alter the contents of the budget, it will also be able to increase it within certain limits. . . .

The increase in the communities' activities, the decision to give the community an independent budget, and the increased powers of the European Parliament provided further arguments for the election of the parliament by direct universal suffrage. The summit conference in Paris in October 1972 discussed this at length, but without reaching agreement. The debate will doubtless be resumed in connection with the target of a "European union" by 1980 set at the summit, quite apart from other possible initiatives. Moreover, several national parliaments are considering bills providing for their own countries' delegates to the European Parliament to be directly elected, without waiting for the election by this means of the parliament as a whole.

PARLIAMENT:
THE "UNHATCHED INSTITUTION" [4]

"Europe is dying," three Common Market commissioners told the French Senate last month.

The bold and noble dreams that galvanized the peoples of Western Europe after World War II appear to be disintegrating, with the region's nations in increasing disarray individually and collectively.

The weakness is most dramatically visible in Strasbourg, home of the European Parliament.

Imagine a United States Congress whose members can advise but neither consent to nor pass laws, who belong both to their state legislatures and the national body, who speak six different languages and spring from nine distinct countries.

[4] From "Strasbourg Parliament Shows Weakness of Europe," by Nan Robertson, staff correspondent, Paris bureau. New York *Times*. p 2. Mr. 11, '74. © 1974 by The New York Times Company. Reprinted by permission.

Miracle and Dilemma

This is both the miracle and the dilemma of the Common Market's European Parliament, whose members are grouped not by states but by their politics from Communist to conservative.

Their latest session ended in Strasbourg in open soul-searching about the future of the Common Market and the fate of the 250 million citizens in its nine countries.

The 198 delegates to the European Parliament sit in their national legislatures, which select them to go to Strasbourg. Members of the body in six of the nine nations—Britain, West Germany, Italy, Belgium, the Netherlands and Luxembourg—are working for direct elections to the Strasbourg assembly. The French, the Danes and the Irish are hanging back.

Market's Sole Public Forum

A popular mandate could allow this feeble but democratic debating society to speak with the voters' voices and transform it into a Europe-wide political force. For now it is an "unhatched institution," as one observer put it, adding, "The egg is there, but the chick hasn't been allowed to peck through."

Nowhere is the picture of a Europe divided and diverse yet longing to speak with one voice projected more dramatically than in the European Parliament. It is the Common Market's only public forum, in contrast with other market groupings, in which the horse-trading is done in private and communiqués are issued at the end.

The parliament meets on an average of once a month in Europe House, a low, dingy concrete structure built near the Rhine in 1949 and meant to last only ten years. It became the legislature's home in 1958 when the Common Market was established.

The assembly hall looks like a run-down school gymnasium, with strip windows near the ceiling on two sides,

dirty Venetian blinds, pale aquamarine tiles on the walls
and amphitheater seating for the delegates. . . .

Everywhere there is paper, tons of it, piled on the delegates' desks and on press room tables and tacked to bulletin
boards. Each report—or *rapport, relazione, bericht, verslag,
betænkning*—is color-coded in six languages for instant recognition.

All English translations are printed on fuchsia paper,
Dutch is orange, German yellow, Italian green, Danish pink
and French pale blue. No speech, no amendment, no resolution, no correction to any resolution, no cancellation of
any such correction goes unrecorded, six times over.

The Ushers Are Splendid

All alone on one sheet of fuchsia paper, picked at ran-
dom from a pile, was this embodiment of a policy change:
"Improvement of the Common Agricultural Policy [CAP].
Motion for a resolution. Paragraph one. In the first line of
this paragraph, replace the word 'welcomes' by the word
'notes.' " . . .

Members Get Around

The delegates, as in Congress, doze, read newspapers and
reports, write letters, scratch and wander about. This practice of wandering about surprised a group of British tourists,
who said that although their lawmakers make a lot of noise
and have honed the art of the shouted, nasty quip, "They
generally stay more or less put."

The permanent background noise of the European Parliament is the gabbling undertone of the instantaneous interpreters, perched in glass-fronted control booths along the
front wall. This filters through the earphones at every seat.

There are sixty interpreters, and the favorite seems to be
the wildly gesturing woman who interprets German speak-
ers for Italians.

All agree that the delegates from Britain, which entered
the Common Market a year ago along with Denmark and

the Irish republic and represent the most powerful and ancient parliament of the nine nations, have injected a new vigor into the institution. The British have added political bite to technical and tactical discussions.

With their addition, a question period was also introduced on a wide range of current topics. On a recent day, debate ranged from the plight of [Russian author] Aleksandr I. Solzhenitsyn to why the European Parliament will have nothing to do with the Greeks. Athens, said one delegate [referring to the military regime then in power], has "no parliament worthy of the name."

But the strongest theme running throughout the entire session was the worry about Europe and where Europe was going. Members spoke of "brutal change and transformation" of the union battered by a "hurricane" of events in 1973—war in the Middle East, monetary chaos, national egotism, superpower snubs, oil up for grabs at four times the price of several months before.

Again and again, in different tongues and from every stripe of the political spectrum, delegates from the nine countries expressed their fears that earnestly sought cohesion, welded during fifteen years of economic boom, was disintegrating.

"Cooperation is easy enough in good times," said Sir John Peel, a Conservative member of the House of Commons. "Now we are entering a crucial test of the European ideal."

Makeup of the Market

The majority of those sitting in Strasbourg represents the stanchly pro-European segments of their own national legislatures.

They are frustrated by their inability to cement European union because they are institutionally barred from doing so.

The Common Market functions on three levels. The executive Commission—thirteen international civil servants

picked through agreement of the nine member governments
—proposes. The parliament discusses. The Council of Ministers decides.

All the power of the Common Market is vested in the
Council of Ministers, which acts on work prepared by the
market's Commission in Brussels. Yet the European Parliament goes on, asking questions, venturing opinions, hoping
for more power. Its budget is $30 million a year, provided
by the taxpayers of the nine countries.

"Do you know what it is?" said Roger Broad, a staff
member of the European Parliament for a decade. "It's taxa-
tion without representation."

THE EUROCRATS OF BRUSSELS [5]

When Britain signs the treaty of accession to the European communities this weekend [January 22, 1972], it will
also be agreeing to become involved in what has variously
been described as "a monstrous bureaucracy," "a toothless
wonder" and "the finest collection of governing technocrats
in the world"—the European Commission in Brussels. Who
runs this Commission, and how much do they matter?

The Commission has three main functions in the EEC.
It is, first, a political animal. Its nine commissioners [now
thirteen] have the sole collective right to put new policies
up to the EEC's chief decision makers, the Council of Ministers, who represent the individual member governments.

Secondly, the Commission issues regulations for the community as a whole. This includes telling individual member
states to get into line on matters that they have all previously agreed to, either under the Treaty of Rome or under
subsequent decisions reached by the Council of Ministers.

Thirdly, the Commission is a straight bureaucracy. It
polices the EEC's customs union and its rules for free movement of labor; it administers the mammoth common farm

⁵ From "Who's Afraid of the European Commission?" *Economist* (London).
242:52. Ja. 22, '72. Reprinted by permission.

policy and makes annual proposals on farm prices; and it acts as a European monopolies commission, with powers (which it uses somewhat sporadically) to check mergers, cartels and selling arrangements which in its opinion inhibit competition. Governments, companies and individuals have the right of appeal against all its rulings to the Court of Justice in Luxembourg.

The Commission thus has a big bailiwick, which it runs with about six thousand people—a fifth of the size of Britain's department of trade and industry. Like most civil services, it is divided into permanent departments. Some, like agriculture, are big; others . . . do precious little but collect information and issue dust-gathering reports.

On top of this permanent civil service sit the commissioners with their own personally appointed staffs. To a large extent the personality of the Commission depends on these nine [now thirteen] men. . . . Strictly speaking, the Commission members are chosen jointly by all the Common Market governments; in practice each government's candidates are automatically ratified by others.

The commissioners do not serve as representatives of their countries. They are forbidden to take instructions from their own governments, and have to take an oath of independence and loyalty to the community as a whole before taking up office. But the method of selection does mean that individual commissioners owe their jobs to the folks back home, and most spend a good deal of time keeping in touch. This is not necessarily a bad thing; a good commissioner should have the ear of his own government in order to be able to get it to support the Commission's policies.

When commissioners' disputes cannot be solved by referring back to the Treaty of Rome, the job of banging heads falls to the president. The personality of the president is thus becoming increasingly important as the treaty itself is overtaken by events for which it provides no guidance. . . .

President's Powers

Awkwardly, just at this moment when the role of the president of the Commission should have become more important, his status has in fact diminished. Historically, the Commission is the descendant of the High Authority of the coal and steel community, set up under M. Jean Monnet in 1952. M. Monnet enjoyed the full confidence—indeed, the reverence and awe—of all six governments; they allowed him to handpick his own colleagues. This tradition of personal power was carried on by Herr Walter Hallstein, who presided over the EEC Commission from its inception in 1958 until its merger in 1967 with the High Authority and the Euratom Commission. Herr Hallstein, one of the architects of the Treaty of Rome, succeeded in imposing his authority on his colleagues and lent credibility to the idea of the Commission as the nucleus of a future government of an integrated Europe. This infuriated President de Gaulle.

In the end Herr Hallstein went too far. In 1965 the Commission proposed what amounted to a federal budget for the community. President de Gaulle blew up. France boycotted the community for six months. Although the powers of the Commission under the treaty were preserved intact (and Herr Hallstein stayed on), its nerve was broken. Under the Luxembourg compromise which put an end to the 1965 crisis, it was agreed that in future the presidency would be held for only two years, and rotate between member countries. This more or less guaranteed that no future president would be able to establish great personal power.

AND THEN THERE WERE NINE [6]

On January 1 . . . [1973] the independent countries of Britain, Ireland, and Denmark voluntarily gave up some of

[6] From "Europe 1973: Is Another Superpower Emerging?" *Senior Scholastic.* 101:4-6. Ja. 15, '73. Reprinted by permission from *Senior Scholastic,* © 1973 by Scholastic Magazines, Inc.

their independence. They became, officially, members of the European Economic Community, or the Common Market.

Initially the step itself makes few demands. Many elaborate documents are signed with appropriate pomp. Here and there a tariff—a tax placed on a product being brought across a border—is lowered.

Far more significant is that these three nations have committed themselves to a basic idea. That is, they must join the six other nations of the Common Market—Italy, France, West Germany, Luxembourg, Belgium, and the Netherlands —in a common economic bond. In pooling their commercial resources they have agreed that together they can create a better life for their people than they could do on their own. And in doing so they have also, by implication, laid the groundwork for a potential political union—a union that may one day make most of Europe one nation.

"This is the Year of Europe," said Henry Kissinger. . . .

He has a point. Behind the rhetoric which economists and other technocrats have spun, one thing is already apparent. The union of the three with the original six of the Common Market has created the world's third superpower. From the windswept Shetland Islands in the Norwegian Sea to the tip of the Italian boot it has linked 250 million people in a common bond.

A New Giant

Any way you measure it, the Common Market is a force to be reckoned with. That population of 250 million people is larger than that of either the United States or the Soviet Union. Its Gross National Product (the value of all goods and services) is more than $700 billion. That's about $300 billion below the US figure.

Even before the three new members joined, EEC exports to the outside world totaled $55 billion. US exports, meanwhile, figured around $43 billion.

Furthermore, the original six-member EEC was second

only to the United States in automobile manufacturing. It was the world's third largest producer of steel. And one of the world's most important agricultural producers.

Now, as a nine-member market, it will be bigger and stronger than ever. Just how this new bloc will affect relations with other countries is the question government officials the world over are asking themselves.

Common Market members have yet to work out many details of how trade with other countries will be handled. But one thing is already clear. Nonmembers will have to deal with the nine-member bloc as a whole. In a statement issued last October EEC officials said:

"The conference reaffirmed its determination to follow a common commercial policy toward the countries of Eastern Europe starting January 1, 1973."

Comrade Capitalist

The reason for such careful statement of policy so early is because the stakes are huge. Trade with the Communist countries has grown tremendously since the Common Market first opened shop in 1958. That year trade with the Soviet bloc added up to $1.3 billion. In 1971, the figure was $6.8 billion. Imports from East Europe rose by more than *300 percent* during those years. Food, beverages, tobacco, and other raw materials accounted for the biggest individual share of those sales.

Western Europeans, meanwhile, are sending manufactured goods eastward. Things like ships, electrical machinery, and textiles. The flow of these goods into the iron curtain grew by more than 400 percent in the same years.

If anything this trade will probably increase now. Each side has goods the other wants. And neither side is letting political ideas get in the way of doing business. As Soviet leader Leonid Brezhnev said at a meeting of Soviet workers, the European Economic Community is "a fact of life."

Where Does the United States Fit In?

The answer depends on just who it is you're asking. Some Americans are clearly upset by Common Market policies. A major sore point is the special trade deals worked out between the EEC and dozens of other countries around the world.

The "preferential trade area," as it's called, is made up mostly of ex-colonies of the European member countries. Britain's special ties to its many Commonwealth nations. France's link to its former African colonies. All of them form yet another, even larger, union.

The problem is that US goods are discriminated against within this area. In contrast to EEC goods, the American products must pay extra taxes. This makes the US goods costlier—and less competitive—than the EEC products.

"Important elements in the business community, labor and the Congress," says a US trade expert, "are becoming increasingly impatient with a system in which certain countries can deny our exports the same terms they offer [others]."

The biggest headache is in the area of farm products. US farm exports to the original six Common Market nations dropped by 20 percent between 1966 and the end of 1971. It happened because high tariff fees added to the price of US goods sold in Europe. Inside the Common Market, products of European farms are usually cheaper than those in the United States. . . .

The Europeans, of course, are quick to point out that there are two sides to every argument. Sales of US *nonfarm* products to the EEC have been growing by about 9 percent a year. In 1971 these exports totaled more than $7 billion, or $1.28 billion more than we bought from them.

There are some people who think the enlarged Common Market could be a bonanza for the United States. In the past, different industrial standards, product testing requirements, etc., were often a major hurdle for American firms.

With uniform regulations covering all nine countries this technical barrier may be eased.

"The Common Market is the new frontier for American industry, its promised land," says Jean-Jacques Servan-Schreiber. Servan-Schreiber, editor of the respected French magazine, *l'Express,* is an expert on United States-European business. His book, *The American Challenge,* is an authoritative study of the reasons for US business success in Europe.

Man in the Street

"I believe in Europe, but not in the Common Market," a young bearded Dane told an American correspondent.

"The young are losing interest in EEC. We here (at the Brussels headquarters) live in an ivory tower." That was Sicco Mansholt, a Dutchman and [former] president of the EEC Commission talking.

Is it true? Is all the high finance winging back and forth way out of sight of the average man or woman on the street?

Facts from the European Community Information Service shed some light on the situation. There's still a lot of work to be done in the EEC. Special taxes, distribution costs, and other regulations won't completely disappear for another several years. And that can mean higher prices for the average person.

Clothing prices, for example, can still differ by as much as 35 percent from one EEC country to the next. Medicine prices can vary by as much as 72 percent.

On the other hand, Europeans today have a wider range of goods available than they did back in 1958. Two examples: The availability of foreign-made clothing is much higher today than in 1958. The same is true when it comes to buying a family car. Those increased sales naturally are reflected in the job market in each country.

Although Europe is going through a time of serious inflation, life is better for the average person. The consumer within the EEC has increased his consumption of all goods by 72 percent in the last fourteen years. And total consumer spending has risen by 92 percent in the Common Market countries. That compares with a 35 percent increase in the United States and 38 percent in Britain.

1972: END OF AN ERA [7]

The world became a smaller place in 1972, but Western Europe became a little bigger. The globe contracted as the United States stepped across iron and bamboo frontiers to search for sounder economic and political relationships with the Soviet Union and China.

The European Economic Community, or Common Market, reached out to the lands on its periphery giving it not only a new geographic dimension but also a political and economic weight that could not be ignored.

There was not yet, and perhaps never will be, a grand design for this new Europe to replace the now dated federalist vision of Jean Monnet, Robert Schuman and the Common Market's other founding fathers of the 1950s.

In place of long-range planning, there was impromptu decision making on the basis of short-term political expedients. In place of harmony, there was discord.

The absence of a single power center in the new Europe exasperated those who had to deal with it. It also threatened to keep the Europeans from getting what they said they wanted most: a decisive influence over their own future.

The test was bound to come sooner rather than later because of the intense negotiations on security, trade and monetary matters that were about to begin in the new year as part of an exercise in reshaping the world for the next quarter-century.

There was a tendency in the United States to shrug off

[7] From "Testing Spirit of Community," by Clyde H. Farnsworth, staff correspondent. New York *Times.* p 41-2. Ja. 14, '73. © 1973 by The New York Times Company. Reprinted by permission.

European integration efforts and dismiss the Common Market as being little more than an association of states.

"Without an agenda for Europe, without an articulation of goals and a vague idea of how one wants to achieve them, it would be my notion that Europe will muddle along leaving everyone a bit worse off than could be the case," a young Princeton professor, Edward L. Morse, writes in the . . . [January 1973] issue of *Foreign Affairs.*

The Europeans' view is somewhat different.

First, there seems to be a pretty widespread feeling of almost everyone from London to Munich that a process of unification is under way and is irreversible so long as the globe continues to contract.

Second, there was a profound shock last September [1972] when the Norwegians said no thanks to the invitation to join the Common Market.

The Norwegians were turned off by a number of things, such as a lack of democracy in the club and its emphasis on economic and financial as opposed to social values.

The disenchantment in Norway has led to a fundamental rethinking of the Common Market's goals. One of the positive results is the attention now being paid to the European Parliament in Strasbourg. To give it some real power and influence has become one of the hottest issues on the European agenda. . . .

Up to now the Common Market has been a somewhat frustrating experience for the Germans. While industry has reaped financial rewards, successive Bonn governments have been blocked each time they wanted to strengthen the central institutions of the community. And it was the French who did the blocking.

In addition to internal pressures, external forces are pulling the European Economic Community together.

Henry A. Kissinger . . . has said that . . . [1973] will be the Year of Europe. Europeans are a little worried about what this means. . . .

At a recent diplomatic luncheon in Paris, a high officer

of the French foreign ministry quipped, "I hope the United States is good and tough because a good scrap is what we need to make Europe."

There are two or three main points of economic conflict that will be hard to resolve because of fundamental differences in philosophy.

One is the linkage of preferential trade agreements built up between the Common Market's core area and its periphery in Europe and North Africa. . . .

Another point of conflict is the community's protectionist farm policy. This tends to keep out or at least limit imports of food products from the big food-exporting countries such as the United States, Canada and Australia. The policy is intended to help poor farmers.

What the United States says is that other countries should not be required to pay for the Common Market's social programs, especially when the member countries are rich enough to pay the bills themselves. But a common farm policy represents one of the few areas where the Common Market countries have been able to merge their interests. So the attacks of the United States look to Europeans as if Washington is trying to undermine European unity.

Similar expressions were heard from Europeans when the United States proposed, as a long-term objective, the elimination of tariffs on industrial goods by the trading nations.

The common external tariff of the European Economic Community is another form of cement that keeps the member states together.

Against these American challenges, the Europeans are being compelled, if they want to keep their community alive, to get together in other fields. Money is the sector where the most work has been done. If the monetary experiments succeed, defense will follow. . . .

Only by intermingling resources, many observers feel, will the Europeans be able to deal with their greatest internal problem: to narrow the regional and social differences in the community. And only by intermingling resources will they be able to speak with a single voice in the great international monetary, trade and security debates.

II.   A TUMULTUOUS TRANSITION

EDITOR'S INTRODUCTION

The process of integrating the community's three new members, even in more or less normal times, would have entailed a long period of adjustment. But few anticipated the turbulence that actually accompanied the first months of transition: a war in the Middle East, monetary instability, rampant inflation, and differences with the United States. By 1974 the Common Market, in the words of European Commission President François-Xavier Ortoli, was in a "state of crisis—a crisis of confidence, of will, and of clarity of purpose." The dimensions of the crisis are detailed by Flora Lewis, Paris bureau chief of the New York *Times,* in this sections's first article.

The crisis prompted Europeans to take fresh stock of the Common Market, where it was and where it was going. Jan G. Reifenberg, a German correspondent stationed in Washington, finds cause for optimism in the emergence of two new pragmatic leaders, West Germany's Helmut Schmidt and France's Valéry Giscard d'Estaing. The generally pro–Common Market *Economist* takes a more somber view.

In the winter of their discontent, the Common Market's leaders held a summit meeting in Copenhagen and reaffirmed their dedication to European unity. These were brave words, but according to the *Wall Street Journal*'s Richard F. Janssen, the unity drive had, in fact, slowed down.

A STATE OF CRISIS [1]

A habit has developed here [in Brussels] at the head-quarters of the European Economic Community [EEC or Common Market] of shouting "crisis!" as often as the shepherd cried "wolf!" But suddenly, the international staff of Eurocrats has come to remember that the wolf in the fable did appear and gobble the flock when no one bothered to listen any more.

That is the feeling behind the remarkably plaintive "state of the community" declaration issued by the Common Market's thirteen-member executive Commission . . . [on January 31, 1974], with its warning that the effort to build a united Europe can collapse unless the governments and their peoples act soon to cope with "the challenge facing them."

The texture of the long-familiar Brussels tale of woe has changed with remarkable abruptness.

Only a year ago, the haggles and hostilities were contained in a wrapping of euphoria as Britain, Ireland and Denmark "entered Europe," as joining the community is called. There were grumbles and all-night tugs of war as usual, but they paled beside the sparkling hopes and dazzling charts showing how big, how rich, how resourceful and how weighty the expanded community had become.

The Climate Has Reversed

Only a half a year ago, there were outbursts of self-congratulation as the diplomats of the community, faced with an American call for a "new Atlantic Charter," answered

[1] From "Europe's 9 Looking Hard at Their 'Crisis,'" by Flora Lewis, chief, Paris bureau. New York *Times*. p 8. F. 2, '74. © 1974 by The New York Times Company. Reprinted by permission.

with "a single voice," expressing the Common Market's will to meet America as a political equal.

Now, the climate has reversed. There is virtual unanimity among the Eurocrats, including Frenchmen, but their harmony is a lament. Government representatives seem only a few degrees less apprehensive that the "Europe" of words may never become a "Europe" of deeds, except perhaps for the French who have their own ideas.

On all sides, there is talk of the need for a bold move, a firm step, a new surge lest the whole ambitious notion falter.

The Commission's urgent cry for action specified the community's behavior at the Washington conference of oil-consuming nations February 11 [1974] as a "test" of its will to act as a real community.

And yet, the Commission was working today on a proposal for the foreign ministers of the nine countries to consider next week what, by present indications, seems likely to be a watery, evasive compromise.

But compromise, commissioners and diplomats explained, is necessarily the way of life in the community, and anything more than an expressed willingness to hear Washington's views might reveal with too much public drama what all know: The gap of disagreement on substance is too wide to be covered by something no more solid than procedural paper.

A Crisis of Method

What has gone wrong so fast? Officials within and without the community's bureaucracy make their analyses in various ways, reflecting their national and personal backgrounds. But whether they work behind the glass walls of the Commission's modern beehive building or in a number of embassies, the themes are surprisingly the same.

First, all say that it is a crisis of institutions, of method, of capacity. Urgent decisions are pressing and there is no way to get decisions made. The Commission has not the power and the governments have not shown the will.

The reason for that, more than one official said with distress, is that governments no longer really believe community action fulfills their purposes better than individual national action.

The immediate issues now, huge and frightening, are: the need for a common energy policy; a fund to help the poorer regions of Europe's community so that its people will have more in common; a way to coordinate the crucial decisions of economic policy and money so that the national parts don't strain off in opposite directions of inflation, boom, recession and unemployment, and thus drive countries to close themselves in once more against their neighbors.

The second theme of the Brussels chorus now is that precisely because these issues are so big, so important, they confront the community with a wholly new order of decisions that it has never acquired the power to make.

When the time comes for "a big choice" to be made, one British official said, "You have to go with one or the other, the nation or the community; it is a qualitative leap you always knew would come some day but never prepared yourself to take."

"A Crisis of Enlargement"

The obvious difference in the last year has been the advent of the new members. But Britain is not blamed for the trouble. "It was coming sooner or later, the British may just have speeded the impact and the visibility," said a West German, and Frenchmen, Belgians, Italians echoed the view.

"It is a crisis of enlargement," said another Briton, "but it had to come. The French idea of the community was that it existed for the sole benefit of France. Now the Germans won't give the French all their own way anymore, and the British are there to pull for their own needs. It's a new pattern."

Still, nobody in Brussels seems to think that it is too late to save the community. Its capital is alive with plans for reform, for dramatic appeals to create a new determination to press toward unity. . . .

There is an idea of creating a European cabinet with defined and delegated powers of decision from national governments. There is an idea of some kind of spectacular appeal over the heads of governments to the powerless European Parliament and the indifferent publics.

These ideas all have a quality of fevered fantasy, and this is quickly admitted. But while people here say that there no longer are inspiring leaders like the late Robert Schuman of France or Konrad Adenauer of West Germany to make the doubters act by the power of their own belief, there still appears to be an ardent wish that keeps things going.

"Crises bring forth their men," said a Frenchman.

"Mediocre men can fall off the fence into greatness despite themselves, if they are pushed," said an Englishman.

Their words seemed to underline how different the current crisis is.

Underneath there seemed to be a sense that among the people of the community's member countries "Europe" is not much of an issue. And that, the Eurocrats say, is because "Europe" has not actually shown that it can solve problems better as a unit than its members can individually.

The community, it seems, has lost touch with the political forces of its component nations. Many people in Brussels are trying to think up ways to renew contact, and that was the meaning and the purpose of the Commission's cry of "crisis!"

NEW PRAGMATIC LEADERSHIP [2]

The age of great personalities and charismatic leaders in Europe is over. Now, the technicians and pragmatists are at work. . . .

[2] From "New Leaders, a New Atlantic Alliance?" by Jan G. Reifenberg, Washington correspondent for the *Frankfurter Allgemeine Zeitung. European Community.* 178:19-20. Jl. '74.

In recent months the leaderships of Britain, France, Portugal, and Germany have changed. Italy, in the grips of inflation and political turmoil, had to impose customs barriers within the community, Denmark reduced its imports, the British Labour government demands renegotiation of its hard-earned terms of entry, and France floated its currency. Some of these steps are technically breaches of the Common Market treaty.

An Era Ends

Yet, all of this has not jolted Western Europe into chaos but merely underscored the transitional period in which we all live. It is also proof of a large undercurrent of social and economic awareness, a trend which began during the sixties as the "classic" cold war abated and the effects of an affluent society were challenged. It is a consequence of the sense of realism which asserted itself after the confrontation between the United States and the Soviet Union during the Cuban missile crisis of October 1962—the limits of power had been shown and proven. It is also a consequence of the conscientious reducing of America's overextension of power, symbolized by its withdrawal from the war in Vietnam.

An era ended when German Chancellor Willy Brandt resigned in the wake of a sordid spy scandal, which seemed to put a dismal finish to a courageous, farsighted, and noble career. The Europe of today would not be possible if the Federal Republic, under Brandt and his Foreign Minister Walter Scheel, had not drawn the lessons from World War II and recognized that Bonn had a responsibility, indeed an obligation, to come to terms with its Eastern neighbors, upon whom the most terrible wounds of the last European war were inflicted. Until a modus vivendi was reached with East Germany, until the Berlin problem was defused and the livelihood of the Western part of the city guaranteed, until the relations with the Soviet Union, Poland, Czechoslovakia, and the other East European countries were normalized, the "German problem" remained the biggest danger to Europe. When the wall between the two parts of Berlin went up in August 1961, and the United States—out of its sense of nuclear responsibility did not move (as it had not moved during the East German revolt of 1953 and the Hungarian rebellion of 1956)—West Berlin Mayor Brandt recognized the necessity for change from the cold war.

German Chancellor Konrad Adenauer's monument in time will be Germany's rehabilitation, its membership in the Western alliances, and its reconciliation with France, the futile dream of Gustav Stresemann and Aristide Briand of the late twenties finally come true. Willy Brandt's monument will be the act of courage that it took to begin to overcome the wall of mistrust separating East and West and to recognize the facts, painful as they are for a divided people. Kneeling in front of the monument to the victims and martyrs of Warsaw's razed ghetto took at least as much courage as praying—which Adenauer did—next to de Gaulle in the cathedral of Rheims, yards away from the red schoolhouse where Hitler's armies surrendered. The fact that détente progresses slowly, that the resigned chancellor was largely deceived by East Germany's hard attitude and finally driven out of office by the presence of one of its agents in his official family will not change the significance of Brandt's *Ostpolitik* [conciliatory policy toward Russia and its allies] for Europe.

Eye-to-Eye

But very real and pressing domestic and economic problems also contributed to Brandt's resignation. Inflation, although presently at 7 percent one of the lowest in the West, remains to most Germans a horror because of the experiences of their fathers in the twenties. Too, the chancellor was apparently unable to come to grips with the extreme leftist elements in his Social Democratic party. And international problems spilled over into the domestic arena: While in the forties and fifties, the danger of Soviet intrusion fostered Western unity, by late 1973, the Mideast war brutally revealed Germany's and Western Europe's dependence upon Arab oil and a potential Western split.

For the future of Western Europe, the community, and transatlantic relations, it is highly significant that the two new leaders of France and Germany, President Valéry Giscard d'Estaing and Chancellor Helmut Schmidt, not only know and esteem each other personally but see eye-to-eye on most pressing problems. Both are pragmatists. Both have a good knowledge of what de Gaulle, often disdainfully, called "the Anglo-Saxons." Both prefer acts to symbols, practical results to dreams. Both have seen and lived through war as young people. Neither is burdened by the past nor feels bound to prove his country's progress by constantly referring to past glories or tragedies. Both understand well what the computer age, the all-pervasiveness of the energy problem, the transnational economic and monetary realities, mean. Both realize that the youth of their countries are fed up with symbolism and want results. Both preside over cabinets whose members are representative of the postwar generation.

Giscard d'Estaing and Schmidt are thus a distinct hope for the future of the community. French and German policy coordination will decisively influence the community's course, especially since Britain has a long way to overcome its present economic problems. The late French President Georges Pompidou never shed an inborn distrust of Germany. His *rapprochement* with former British Prime Minister Edward Heath and the lifting of France's veto against UK entrance into the community was one of its consequences. But, as in de Gaulle's days, it proved impossible to make France the factual political leader in Western Europe and Germany mainly its "economic locomotive." The realities are different and were proven by *Ostpolitik*.

Giscard d'Estaing and Schmidt have a broader outlook. They are less afraid of losing national identities through closer economic, monetary, and finally, political cooperation. Born in this century, tempered by war, grown up in the postwar world, both have always seen Winston Churchill's 1946 prophetic demand for European political union and Franco-German reconciliation as a challenge for practical work.

A "NOT QUITE EMPTY" WAREHOUSE [3]

When . . . [British Foreign Secretary James] Callaghan goes to Luxembourg to spell out the changes Britain wants in the Common Market next Tuesday [June 4, 1974] he will be talking to a Europe that has radically changed its shape since the overblown pretensions of a year ago, and has changed even since he first lectured it in early April. European and Atlantic unity both now resemble not quite empty warehouses: fair buildings with little inside. Each month a little more stock is sold from the free trade storehouse of the European Economic Community without being replaced. The NATO [North Atlantic Treaty Organization] alliance itself goes unchallenged, but its political capital is eroded by European members who nibble away at forms of words to describe Atlantic unity as though no danger existed that the United States might give up and go away.

So the meeting this weekend of Europe's two new masters, [German Chancellor] Helmut Schmidt and [French President] Valéry Giscard d'Estaing, is well timed to redefine the possibilities of Europe. But the trust which these two men happen to have in each other will not be enough to let them say where Europe goes next. The best that they can fashion in the EEC itself is a survival kit. . . . Events are the present masters of Europe, not men. The damage to the customs union and the farm policy of the EEC is likely to get worse before it even has a hope of getting better.

[3] From "The Trimline New Europe." *Economist* (London). 251:14-15. Je. 1, '74. Reprinted by permission.

For Both the Do-Cares and the Don't-Cares

If they wish to look forward, therefore, M. Giscard d'Estaing and Herr Schmidt will first have to look back. The turning point in Europe's fortune was the Paris summit meeting of the nine in October, 1972. The outcome of that Paris meeting was the sum of the good intentions of every member state. Of course, good intentions are necessary to any project, but they are not enough; and this lot has been shaken to bits by what has happened since. The sixteen chapters of that summit declaration nearly two years ago prescribed a timetable for economic and monetary union (EMU) in Europe, for EEC regional, social, industrial, energy and environment policies; and they dictated a more outward-looking trade and external policy. On every single one of these headings, except for a few modest steps to monitor pollution together, the nine have moved backwards, not forwards.

Two conditions of political life in 1972 gave rise to that abortive summit message. One reason for the summit was the don't-care attitude of Europe's young—about orthodox national party politics, about defense, even about the nature of society in the illiberal regimes of East Germany and Russia. [French President] Georges Pompidou (now dead), [German Chancellor] Willy Brandt (resigned) and [British Prime Minister] Edward Heath (defeated) each personally and genuinely believed that a new direction could be given to national affairs by, among other things, binding them to a wider European purpose. This purpose, though expressed in EEC jargon, would with time, it was thought, prove to be demonstrably grand (EMU and political union); demonstrably humane (regional and social policy); demonstrably modern (industrial and environment policy); and demonstrably outward-looking.

The second parent of that Paris summit was the do-care generation. Most Europeans over the age of thirty—those whose memories date back to sweet rationing and not having a family car in the 1940s—do care very much (perhaps too much) about becoming richer again next year, and richer still the year after that. By 1972 the EEC's real rate of growth, its chief glory in the 1960s, was slowing dangerously down. Its rate of inflation was speeding dangerously up. The whole logic of the EEC for the do-care generation suggested that this was the moment, with Britain at last about to join, for a step forward. For without a step forward, as has in fact subsequently happened, the EEC could only step back. By 1972 the customs union was running out of steam. Growth was hampered by nontariff barriers, by legal blocks to cross-frontier industry, by lack of real European social and regional aids. If all these could be remedied, growth could be given a new, regionally balanced upward twist, leading ultimately to economic union of a still undefined sort.

What went wrong? For a start, that Europe of the dreams of 1972 was not the young's Europe. More serious, inflation made sure even before the oil payments crisis that it would not be the Europe of the middle-aged and old either. Each government in Europe now takes whichever short-term national tack will best keep alive the illusion that growth continues for those plump generations which are the foundation of every European government's power.

One other wrecking event has happened in Europe since the summit of 1972. Britain entered the EEC as the only member other than Denmark not to enjoy multiparty support for the idea of joining at all. The Labour party's decision to challenge Britain's entry into the EEC two years ago was regrettable for many reasons, but it happened, and British public opinion did not reject it. Until that knot can be unknotted—either by getting out, or by a successful renegotiation and a referendum—it is unlikely that any British government of any party can be an even half-helpful EEC partner to the rest.

With so much gone wrong in Europe, it would not be harsh of Herr Schmidt and President Giscard d'Estaing to

decide that Britain can go hang. That is the risk which
. . . [Prime Minister Harold] Wilson and Mr. Callaghan,
for Labour party reasons, are now running. If Britain left,
the remaining EEC members would be left with worse farm
surpluses than before—and with more money to find for the
EEC budget. But the fact that several important men in
Bonn and Paris now openly entertain the idea of letting
Britain go illustrates some decisive changes in Europe which
need to be understood.

The first large change since Britain joined [in January
1973] is that Britain no longer matters in the community
all that much except to the extent that it makes every existing EEC problem worse. The balance of power has swung
decisively to France and Germany since the Schmidt era
began in December [1973] over the regional fund and the
energy affair. And it has swung in particular to Germany,
which has at last cast off its foreign policy shackles.

The second change in the past two years is that the need
for a down-to-earth EEC based on its original principles
grows more obvious as the strains on Europe become more
intense. That is why Herr Schmidt, a charter European, is
now trying, in his very hard-edged way, to put a corset
around the free-trading side of the EEC as it exists. Herr
Schmidt's quarrel with the EEC has been with its expensive
ambitions and with its frightful Brussels rigmarole. It has
not been with the trading and foreign policy sides of the
EEC as such. He is now under heavy pressure from Germany's industrialists, its trade unions and the farmers of
Bavaria to shore up what already exists. Much the same
goes for M. Giscard d'Estaing and every other European
government. The faster they run away from integration in
the face of the economic storm, the harder they are being
pressed to stop.

To Avoid a Double Recession

For a few months yet, perhaps longer, little in Europe
will improve whatever Herr Schmidt says. As a result a wel-

come humility should enter into relations between the nine and the United States; although, with so many other pressures on him, M. Giscard d'Estaing will not quickly relinquish the vote-winning Gaullist habit of sticking the occasional pin in America even though it is personally distasteful to him. But the more the nine dismantle the rules of the EEC, the more they will find themselves adding an internal European recession to the recession and inflation which have been wished on them from outside. An economic disaster in Europe could then occur. No one yet knows how much, if any, of the Paris summit charter the nine—or the eight or the seven—will at that grim moment decide to revive. Probably not much. But that they will decide to restore the basic economic aims of the Treaty of Rome—free trade with a social edge and a common foreign trade policy—there can be little doubt. They will do it whether Britain is with them or not. And with Britain in an even worse mess than the rest, it still needs to be in the modest Europe that Mr. Callaghan can help to preserve.

A CRITICAL SUMMIT [4]

Graphic illustration of the winter facing Europe came with the blizzard that hit Copenhagen December 14-15 [1973] during the first of what promises to be many "fireside summits" of the EC [European Community] heads of state or government. The Copenhagen streets were blowing with snow and, except for taxis and buses, were bare of traffic. Danes shivered in homes without hot water. British Prime Minister Edward Heath had, just before his departure for Copenhagen, announced on television that heavy power cuts would have to be made and industrial workweeks reduced.

In these circumstances, the summit's call for the EC Council of Ministers to decide in principle, by the end of February [1974], on proposals "to ensure the orderly func-

[4] From "First 'Fireside Summit.'" *European Community*. 173:6-8. F. '74.

tioning of the Common Market for energy" was none too soon. Other circumstances included four Arab foreign ministers, whose presence in Copenhagen seemed to accord the European Community a degree of recognition and solidarity often not invested by even its friends.

Was the summit a success? Certainly it had not been a flop. Only the week before a story in the Belgian newspaper *Le Soir* said the summit would be playing for "double or nothing," that the community was poised on the brink of collapse or resurrection. By the summit's end, this point had been safely passed. But the real answer lies ahead, in whether the ten-point statement agreed to by the nine is achieved. . . .

Toward a European Identity

In the statement's first point, the nine affirmed "their common will that Europe should speak with one voice in important world affairs." Toward this end, the nine adopted a "declaration on the European identity" which, while keeping in mind the community's "dynamic nature," defines principles for future action. . . .

Toward European Union

The second point in . . . [the] statement said that the nine had agreed to speed up work toward achieving European union by 1980. This goal was first set at the Paris summit in October 1972, when the nine said they intended "to transform the whole complex of their relations into a European union."

Third, the heads of government or state decided to meet more frequently. "These meetings will be held whenever justified by the circumstances and when it appears necessary to provide a stimulus or to lay down further guidelines for the construction of a united Europe . . . [and] whenever the international situation so requires." The initiative for such meetings was left to the EC member state holding the rotating office of president of the EC Council of Ministers at the time. In 1974, the office falls to Germany. . . .

Fourth, the EC member states' foreign ministers were called upon to establish a common procedure for handling crisis situations, such as the recent Mideast and attendant energy crisis.

Fifth, the nine "confirmed their support for the policy of international détente which respects the independence and security of each state and the rules laid down in the charter of the United Nations for the prevention and settlement of conflicts."

Sixth, the nine agreed that their "growing unity would strengthen the West as a whole and will be beneficial for the relationship between Europe and the United States."

Seventh, the heads of state or government "welcomed the convening of a peace conference [on the Middle East] in Geneva and called on the participants to make every effort to achieve a just and lasting settlement at an early date. . . ."

Eighth, the heads of state or government called for more rapid progress toward full economic and monetary union. In particular, they called for a common position on international monetary reform, increased instruments at the disposal of the European Monetary Cooperation Fund, and strengthened coordination to create capital stability in Europe. Regional development policy, strengthened EC institutions, social policy, international trade in primary and raw material, and a common policy for industry, science, and technology also received attention from the nine heads of government or state.

Ninth, the question of energy was deemed so important that the nine released a separate statement on the subject.

Tenth and finally, the heads of state or government said they were "convinced that a united Europe will be able to play a role consonant with its history and its abilities in the service of economic and social progress in the community, of the growth and industrialization of developing countries, and of peace between all nations."

UNITY DRIVE SLOWS [5]

Western Europe is stumbling into a chill and uncertain future despite the potentially historic summit meeting of the political leaders of the nine member nations of the Common Market.

The Arab oil embargo against Holland is what brought the European Common Market to its most important cross-roads since the Treaty of Rome created the community in 1958. The starkest choice confronting the nine leaders who met here [in Copenhagen] over the weekend was whether to let Holland suffer alone as if there weren't any Common Market at all or whether to share supplies in a bold show of "solidarity" that would risk more severe sacrifices in the other eight member nations.

Their decision typifies the kind of action that is reducing the flame of European unity to an uninspiring flicker. In effect, that decision was to remain in the relative comfort of the crossroads for as long as possible—rather than making any bold choices now.

While professing full awareness of the "grave" impact that a prolonged oil shortage could have, the nine leaders decided only to seek statistics by January 15, staff proposals by the end of January, and decisions by foreign ministers on orderly energy markets "in principle" before next February 28. Short-run problems of consumer countries were shunted aside for "study" to the Paris-based Organization for Economic Cooperation and Development, a wider forum that hasn't been able to agree on oil either.

No Open Dissents

It is possible, of course, that the leaders who skipped a scheduled news conference with six hundred reporters secretly reached more substantive agreements. One insider

[5] Reprint of "Common Market Delay on Oil Decision Signals Slowing of Unity Drive," by Richard F. Janssen, staff reporter. *Wall Street Journal.* p 1+. D. 17, '73. Reprinted with permission of The Wall Street Journal © 1973 Dow Jones & Company, Inc. All Rights Reserved.

argues that the session was a "success" in the sense that there weren't any open dissents and that the leaders' reaffirmation of the need for "more rapid progress" toward true union at least shows that they aren't giving up.

Perhaps the most favorable omen for a more effective Common Market in the longer run is that the heads of the nine members agree to meet more often and told their foreign ministers to work out a system for reaching decisions "quickly in time of crisis."

However, the lack of immediate and clear decisions on the pressing problem of oil is indicative of what many observers see as the chronic problem of the Common Market. The top political leaders of the member nations find it difficult to come to a consensus without the behind-the-scenes logrolling that characterizes American congressional committees. And the Common Market bureaucracy is getting more deeply embroiled in details that fail to spark European public loyalty.

The Arabs who turned up at the summit didn't make things any easier. "We obviously don't want the nine to align itself with the Dutch position," Tunisian Foreign Minister Mohamed Masmoudi declared. He said the pro-Israeli Dutch themselves strained European solidarity by overlooking the vulnerability of Germany and Belgium to cutoffs of the Arab oil that usually reaches them through the Dutch port of Rotterdam.

The Arab version of how European foreign ministers responded to the Arab message—"play your role" in Mideast diplomacy—sheds some harsh light on Europe's condition. The Tunisian minister said that when the Arabs urged the market nations to be at the Geneva peace talks on the Mideast, the Europeans replied, "No, we can't go, we're powerless." To turn up unbidden would affront the United States, analysts note. And the Common Market admitted only last Friday in its "European identity" statement that there is "no alternative" to dependence on US troops stationed in Europe to shield Europeans from any Soviet encroachment.

The Arabs appeared disappointed at the weekend session despite a Common Market reaffirmation, in strengthened form, of the members' November 6 declaration backing the Arab stand that Israel should withdraw from disputed territories that it occupies.

No Arab Relenting

Any relenting by the Arabs on oil might have taken the Common Market off the hook. But appeals to avert suffering left the Arabs visibly unmoved. Dimming lights and padlocked gasoline stations are nothing compared with the "hundreds of thousands" of drought-stricken Africans starving to death for want of European and American aid, Sudanese Foreign Minister Mansour Kahlid coolly contended. Even "peace in Europe" is at risk unless Europe helps solve the thorny problem of the Palestinian refugees, Algerian Minister Abdelhaziz Bouteflika added ominously.

Passionately held positions by major members of the Common Market had almost assured that the session would be tense—and perhaps crucial to the long-range future of European unity.

"They couldn't have taken an unmitigated disaster" and still expect to make progress on many other matters, one observer said. He added that the hard bargaining went on long enough to avert a shattering schism. But some observers consider the weekend session to have been a "mitigated disaster."

In the weeks leading up to the meeting, Germany played the leading "good-guy" role. Chancellor Willy Brandt rallied the smaller members behind him pushing for "solidarity" with the Dutch—a term taken to mean at least an open expression of support and probably sharing of oil if necessary. Unless the market could stick by a member in dire economic difficulty, the Brandt camp contended, there would be scant hope for maintaining the degree of free trade existing in the market, much less for meeting the chancellor's goal of a single European government sovereign in defense and other key spheres.

The German-led group of seven members and the Brussels Commission staff saw their mission as nothing less than saving the European Economic Community—the formal name of the Common Market. The very name would become a hollow mockery, they feared, if the community didn't seize the opportunity to allocate each member a fair share of oil. Even free-trading Germany would throw up protective barriers against French Renaults, the reasoning went, if France were afloat in oil while Volkswagen slashed output for want of fuel to make or drive cars.

The "bad-guy" role ascribed to Britain and France was undeserved, those governments protested. Instead, their officials argued, they are the ones that have been trying to save the community. If the German-sought "solidarity" had been achieved, British sources said, it would only anger the Arabs into extending their embargo against Holland (and the United States) into an embargo against the entire Common Market. Even the present supply cuts threaten a recession estimated by the market staff at a 2 percent drop in real economic output in 1974, London and Paris noted. So a total embargo would surely bring on a depression that would wreck the community along with many of its member governments, they argued.

Boosting Available Supplies

Because their separate "friendly" gestures to the Arabs promise them a full supply of Arab oil, the British also asserted, they were helping Holland. This paradox comes about, British insiders said, because Britain and France don't have to worsen the frantic scramble for oil from non-Arab producers, such as Nigeria and Iran. Thus, they reasoned, the big international oil companies can continue to clandestinely allocate enough non-Arab oil to spare Holland any real hardship.

France had additional reasons for wanting to stave off oil sharing. "Oil is one form of energy," a Paris aide observes. France hasn't any special reason to share that form with the Dutch, he says, when Holland has rejected the opportunity to take part in a French-led nuclear power project.

Similarly, the British were skittish about setting a precedent that could lead them to share their North Sea oil, which they expect to be abundant by 1980. And they didn't want to give up present oil supplies unless the continent chipped in coal, which is running low because of the British labor dispute.

Against the backdrop of scant movement toward European unity lately, even the general expression of intent to deal with problems "in a concerted manner" was enough to leave the Germans and the Dutch publicly pleased. This was true even though the British and the French could contend that they hadn't given anything away. It may take at least the two and one half months they have allowed themselves before anyone knows which view will prove to be correct.

Holland "Could Get Nasty"

Although small, Holland wasn't altogether helpless. "We could get nasty," one Dutch diplomat threatened in advance, by cutting off the considerable flow of natural gas from Holland to its northern European neighbors. Less dramatically, Holland also hinted that it might toss a monkey wrench into the cumbersome Common Market machinery by blocking the well-advanced plan for "regional development."

The prime ministers did agree to go ahead with this aid to lagging areas by January 1 but couldn't agree on the size and the shape, ordering aides to decide such matters this week.

A specific proposal for more than $2 billion had been drafted and publicized, so the failure to adopt it outright suggests that the plan is caught up in the oil dispute.

Defeat of this aid plan would be especially upsetting to Great Britain, where all of Scotland, Northern Ireland and Wales might qualify and where public dislike of the Common Market is one more handicap for the strike-besieged Heath government. Britons blame the market for soaring food prices (wrongly, the government insists). A recent Common Market poll showed that 33 percent of the British people rate the community as "a bad thing" for them personally. Only 22 percent consider membership good. (In contrast, 54 percent of Italians say the market is good, only 2 percent call it bad.)

Even without the oil crunch, the Common Market was drifting into a quiet crisis of malaise. It was mainly "to inject new momentum and fresh inspiration" into the market that French President Georges Pompidou on October 31 suggested summitry, Danish Prime Minister Anker Jörgensen said Friday. No one doubted that. Despite the stirring commitments made at the Paris summit in October last year, insiders confess, the long march toward a true "European union" by 1980 hasn't left the European public breathless with excitement lately.

Especially since it achieved the long-sought enlargement to nine members last January 1, the community has been losing momentum. Infighting over jobs in the Brussels bureaucracy (Britain fought hard to win the foreign relations post, for example) consumed the first few months of 1973. Then the French went into one of their more prickly nitpicking periods, followed by apprehension that Germany would concoct a crisis to shake the market off dead center.

Before the real crisis came along, the Common Market had gotten down to distinctly unexciting tasks. Tariffs among the original six members (France, Germany, Italy, Belgium, Luxembourg and Holland) are already abolished, and tariffs with the new ones (Great Britain, Ireland and Denmark) are being phased out. So the Brussels Eurocrats have had to turn to tinkering with intricate farm-price props and to tackling technical barriers to free trade. Their "harmonization" proposals, however, seem to have united Europeans mainly in outraged opposition to what's seen at the grass roots as threats to national ways of life.

The biggest little blooper may have been the Eurobeer proposal, intended to let other members export to the thirsty German beer market. At present, they can't because German "cleanliness laws" dating back into the 1500s ban beer that contains anything besides water, barley and hops. Other countries permit the use of wheat, corn, rice and preservative chemicals. To accommodate them, the market proposed a harmonized standard allowing up to 30 percent of grains other than barley.

Perhaps unfairly, the specter of Englishmen giving up their dark warm "bitter" beer and Germany's eighteen hundred local breweries being engulfed by some giant manufacturer of universal and insipid suds caused the idea to die a noisy death. The companion plan for a Euroloaf of standardized bread ingredients was finally abandoned last Friday, bringing cheers from European parliamentarians in Strasbourg.

III. UNFINISHED BUSINESS

EDITOR'S INTRODUCTION

The Common Market has a long and complex agenda to dispose of between now and 1980, the target date for political union. One of the items concerns new members. Roughly half the British population is unhappy with the Common Market. They blame it for everything from high food prices to the weakening of the pound, according to Alvin Shuster, London bureau chief of the New York *Times*. The Labour government has thus begun renegotiating the terms of membership, for reasons spelled out by the *Economist*. Denmark's support for the market, like Britain's, is wavering. Only Ireland, Bowen Northrup of the *Wall Street Journal* reports, appears to be content and prospering.

A second item on the agenda is the Common Agricultural Policy (CAP). Following a brief look at the meaning of the policy, United Press International's Richard C. Longworth details some of the CAP's shortcomings.

Another major European concern is formulating a common energy policy. The need for coordination and cooperation was dramatized by the 1973 oil crisis. *Fortune*'s Lawrence A. Mayer, in three thumbnail sketches, summarizes the effects of that crisis on the economies of Italy, France, and West Germany. Following John Nielsen's look at Europe's overall energy needs and resources, John Walsh, in an article from *Science*, explains why the Common Market members have made very little headway toward a common policy.

The crises and humiliations of 1973-1974 demonstrated the Common Market's weaknesses, but they also underscored some of its strengths, according to James O. Goldsborough, chief European correspondent for the *International Herald*

Tribune. The crises also proved, he believes, that Europe's only hope of maintaining any influence in the world is to move more resolutely toward political union.

"EUROGLOOM" IN BRITAIN [1]

As [former] Prime Minister Heath races his yacht off the English coast, new winds of anxiety are stirring Britain because of an issue that just won't go away—the Common Market [European Economic Community or EEC]. . . .

Seven and a half months after the British formally joined the community officials are still having trouble selling the value of it to a British public that still tends to blame the venture for higher prices and other ills. It has thus been a somewhat trying time for Britain's officials both at home and at market headquarters in Brussels.

The British in general have never been eager about the market. And the experience so far has done little to generate public enthusiasm, largely because visible benefits are hard to come by.

"Unmitigated Loss"

Part of the fresh anxiety over the nine-nation community has been fed by reports from Brussels that senior British civil servants have come to the conclusion that seven months of membership add up to disaster for Britain. The reports have been denied here, but they have nevertheless renewed the debate over whether it was all such a good idea.

Reflecting the trends, one respected British journalist, Samuel Brittan, wrote in the *Financial Times* . . . under the headline "What Changed My Mind About the EEC," "The first seven months of membership have been a pretty well unmitigated loss from this country's point of view."

Aware of public feelings, and the official failure to demonstrate any pluses of membership, British officials last week-

[1] From "Discontent With Common Market Rising in Britain," by Alvin Shuster, chief, London bureau. New York *Times.* p 8. Ag. 15, '73. © 1973 by The New York Times Company. Reprinted by permission.

end sought to put it all in perspective. The seven months may not have ended in disillusion, said John Davies, the minister responsible for market affairs, but they may well have ended in widespread uncertainty.

"I do not think anybody deeply involved in European Economic Community problems would have thought for a moment that the first seven months would be a bonanza," he said.

While expressing unhappiness over the lack of public applause over membership, Mr. Davies said better things were coming. He called the first seven months merely a "preparatory effort."

Heath's View

That has long been the view of Mr. Heath, a devoted European, and his ministers. They argue that the advantages of membership—a higher standard of living, a high growth rate, more exports and the like—would obviously take longer to appear than the drawbacks.

In the meantime, the politicians long opposed to British membership are finding time during this parliamentary recess for a little gloating. They are speaking and writing of the great "disaster" of the market and throwing gloomy statistics around in support of their antimarket stance.

Whatever the figures show—and the government has its own set on economic growth—the public is finding it hard to avoid blaming the community for almost everything, from the jump in the price of bread and other items to the weakening pound, to the subsequent extra charges required for overseas vacations. Although some food prices are leveling off, the food price index itself increased some 7.5 percent from January to June—an annual rate of 15 percent.

Britain's days of cheap food are over. But despite the rise in food prices throughout the world, the British public seems firmly convinced that the trouble stems from the market's Common Agricultural Policy [CAP], which is designed to subsidize community farmers.

"Nothing Is Cheap"

There is a sense that Britain is paying too much into the community to benefit the farmers of France and is unlikely to get commensurate payments from the market's funds to help the poorer regions of Britain. Whatever the facts, there is also a sense that there is too much haggling in Brussels with too few results.

A sampling of opinion around London seems to confirm the present mood over the community.

"There is, of course, some truth about rising food prices in the world," said Mrs. Simone Taylor, a housewife in a London suburb. "But there's no getting away from the fact that nothing is cheap here anymore and I put a large part of the blame for that on our prices being forced into line with those on the continent."

At a rail station in Purley, a south London suburb, Mrs. Ethel Freeman, a housewife, said she was disappointed in the market so far. "The only changes seem to be higher prices and huge continental lorries tearing through our countryside," she said.

"For years I've been advocating the Common Market when most of my friends were against it," said one middle-aged Londoner. "But there's not much to show for it, is there? I have to admit that the French seem more prosperous than ever while we have our wage increases limited and prices are going up all the time."

BRITAIN RENEGOTIATES MEMBERSHIP TERMS [2]

The foreign secretary, Mr. [James] Callaghan, is off to Luxembourg on Tuesday [June 4, 1974] to talk about renegotiating the terms of Britain's membership of the European Economic Community. The argument with the rest of the nine could take up to a year. . . .

If Mr. Callaghan is to make any headway at all the

[2] From "EEC: The British Shopping List." *Economist* (London). 251:66-7. Je. 1, '74. Reprinted by permission.

Europeans will have to be convinced of two things: that the Labour government would prefer to stay in the EEC; and that once the renegotiations are out of the way . . . [Prime Minister Harold] Wilson and Mr. Callaghan will be able to sell EEC membership to the British electorate and make it stick.

The community budget is the biggest issue. Britain believes it is paying in too much and getting out too little. But for the other eight, Italy apart, less from Britain means more from them. This year . . . Britain is contributing a shade over 11 percent . . . Britain gets some money back from the community chest for social spending, farm-fund spending and special subsidies to offset the higher cost of food caused by European currencies appreciating against the pound. But it pays out more than it gets. The EEC budget's net cost to Britain will probably be around £80 million-£100 million this year. It came out a little below the estimated £90 million last year. But compared with Britain's current account deficit, now running at an annual rate of around £4 billion, these sums are peanuts.

The real budget pain starts later. By 1977, Britain's share of the community budget will have moved up in fixed percentage steps to 19.25 percent, following a highly complex formula worked out in . . . [former Prime Minister Edward] Heath's days. After that an automatic revenue system for the community (dreamed up before Britain joined) takes over. But Britain's share will still be held down by a ceiling arrangement which, according to a recent treasury estimate circulated among the nine, still puts the cost to Britain at 23 percent by 1979.

In 1980, all brakes on the new revenue system come off. The snag about this system is that Brussels will automatically pocket all revenues from the common levies on food imported from outside the EEC; from customs duties on other external trade; and from a tax of up to 1 percent on member countries' value added tax base [see Glossary], adjusted to ensure a fair sharing of the burden. Britain would come off worst under this system because it imports a lot from outside the nine.

Some forecasters reckon that Britain could find itself paying nearly 30 percent of the gross community budget in 1980. . . .

That Farm Policy

Britain's second issue is the Common Agricultural Policy (CAP). The CAP, and the effect it has on Britain's access to Commonwealth and other outside suppliers, has been made into a bogey in Britain, and the Labour government continues to make much of it for home audiences. But in Brussels and Luxembourg it is pushing much less hard now.

There are three reasons for this. First, the CAP, unlike the community budget, is already due for renegotiation. For the past six months, the Council of Ministers has had a Commission plan lying on its table containing just the kind of reforms—like plans to avoid food mountains—which, if they were toughened up a bit, Britain would like to see. Second, the Labour government has discovered that CAP price levels and subsidies can be fixed in the council to suit Britain. When it opted out of the EEC's beef price support system altogether its beef farmers were very unhappy.

The third reason for Britain's hopes of getting something on the CAP is the uncertainty about how far world food prices will fall this season, and the even greater uncertainty about what will happen over the next ten years. Grain prices, though falling, are only now sinking to the EEC support buying level. No EEC import levies have had to be paid on American and Canadian wheat coming into Britain this year [1974]. Indeed, for the past year Britain has actually been getting subsidized French grain. . . .

State Aid and EMU

Mr. Callaghan will also raise the question of Brussels's control over what kind of regional and industrial aid the British government may give to British industry. . . .

Mr. Callaghan accepts the need for keeping controls on member states so they do not outbid each other for industry. He objects, however, to doling out more help to run-down farm areas than to run-down industrial ones, and he wants to unravel some of the rules drawn up over the years to make the Brussels control system work. Mr. Heath had already arranged for the system to be rejigged this year. The men who deal with state aid in Brussels are highly pragmatic operators who have already half-agreed among themselves to meet Britain more than half way.

Labour's fears about the EEC's plans . . . leading to full economic and monetary union (EMU) and eventually to political union, have already been reduced by the collapse of the ambitions of two years ago. Mr. Callaghan, if not all his colleagues, has come to realize since his first visit to Luxembourg that there may not be much left of EMU to worry about. Whether or not he will admit as much will depend partly on whether other snags between Britain and its partners will crop up during this awkward year, such as problems over economic or tax policy, import controls or political relations with America. But mostly it will depend on Mr. Callaghan's getting enough to say that Europe has been made fit for Britain to live in.

THE GREENING OF IRELAND [3]

The town of Kinsale, on the coast of County Cork, recently had a parade. The purpose was to commemorate a revolt against the British 372 years ago, but two of the displays had a lot to say about the state of modern Ireland.

First came an old flatbed cart pulled by a donkey. On it, along with a pile of peat, were a clutch of grinning little boys wearing raggedy Irish sweaters and old tweed caps and feigning drunkenness with a number of empty Guinness and

[3] Reprint of "Peat, Donkeys No Longer Symbolize Ireland; Nation Thrives as Common Market Member," by Bowen Northrup, staff reporter. *Wall Street Journal.* p 40. S. 26, '73. Reprinted with permission of The Wall Street Journal © 1973 Dow Jones & Company, Inc. All Rights Reserved.

Irish whisky bottles. They carried a sign reading, "As others see us."

Following directly behind them was a new white Ford containing a smiling and well-scrubbed family of four. They held out two signs, one reading, "As we see ourselves," and the other, "No problem."

Irishmen are getting sick and tired of the old stereotypes, for the simple reason that they no longer apply to most of the three million citizens. Ireland isn't yet rich, but it is taking a quantum jump toward the kind of affluence enjoyed by its fellow members in the European Common Market.

Growing Affluence

By far the biggest element in Ireland's changing face is its membership in the Common Market, now approaching the end of its first year. Ireland is ideally situated to benefit from Common Market programs, particularly the Common Agricultural Policy and the programs for less-developed regions.

Joining Europe has been a psychological boost, too. "They're looking toward Europe as a market," says a foreign observer here.

The signs of growing affluence are widespread. There are many more autos on Ireland's roads now, and many fewer bicycles. On many a rural road, a visitor finds the old stone cottage at one end of a farm—and the farmer putting the finishing touches on a new and bigger house elsewhere on his holding. Dublin is blossoming with boutiques and discothèques—and with big new office buildings. Foreign companies, including many US ones, are setting up plants here to produce for European markets.

The Irish Congress of Trade Unions, which represents about 250,000 workers here, says average weekly earnings of its male members are about $80—not a lot by American standards, but not far below the earnings of their British counterparts (and 14.5 percent above the average last year).

There is progress on other problems. Emigration, the

loss of manpower and talent that has been the curse of modern Ireland, has turned within the past few years into a small net immigration. Tourism, a major industry, is recovering from the blight caused last year by the violence in Northern Ireland. Tourism receipts for the first six months of 1973 were up 12 percent from the year-earlier figure.

But bleak areas remain. The west of the country is badly underdeveloped. Economic equality for women hasn't been achieved. Unemployment, always one of Ireland's chief problems, continues at an unacceptable rate of 7 percent to 8 percent.

Some of the country's problems are directly related to its new prosperity. Inflation for the year ended in May ran at a rate of 11.7 percent, with food prices up a torrid 19.9 percent in the twelve months. The labor unions are getting annoyed about erosion of their earnings.

Basic structural problems have become more evident. Wealth is poorly distributed; a generally accepted estimate is that 5 percent of the people own 70 percent of the wealth. Another "glaring injustice," according to one analyst here: Farmers, and their wives, are exempt from capital gains and income taxes.

This special dispensation stems from the days, not so long ago, when agriculture, inefficiently operated on small family plots, was one of the nation's major problems. Now, with exports to Europe booming, a farmer with a working wife clearly is thriving at the expense of his neighbors.

But a remedy, says this analyst, will be "very tough" for any government to undertake; farmers and their families form the biggest bloc in the Irish electorate.

Squatters and Beggars

Another change is evident, a familiar one in highly industrialized countries: Irish men and women are coming in to the capital from the hinterlands in search of jobs. Thus Dublin has a housing shortage, and the Dublin city commissioners recently were told that there are 488 persons squatting in city-owned housing. Beggars still are common in Dublin.

Forecasts for the economy at large this year are bullish. From 1970 to 1972, the Irish economy had an annual growth rate of only about 3 percent, but, says an official at the department of finance, "We've moved back onto the growth path this year."

The new government, a coalition of the Fine Gael and Labour parties, introduced a record $1.98 billion budget this spring that envisages a 27 percent increase in public expenditures in this fiscal year. The Confederation of Irish Industry recently predicted that the economy would grow by about 6 percent for all of 1973.

"We've had a lot of slack in the economy," says the department of finance official. "This is an export-led expansion —a healthy one." In the first six months of 1973, the Confederation of Irish Industry reports, exports rose by 35.4 percent from the comparable period of 1972.

The export figures demonstrate Ireland's turn toward new markets. Britain always has been its major customer by far. But this year, the industry confederation forecasts, exports to Britain will count for less than half the Irish total for the first time, (not counting Northern Ireland, a British province that takes about 10 percent of the republic's exports).

A major problem for the new government is curbing inflation without curbing growth. It is taking the 5 percent value added tax off food, which may mollify a few housewives. And it has sought to restrain price rises by fixing the profit margins of many wholesalers and retailers. For wage restraint, it relies chiefly on the national wage agreements negotiated by the trade unions with business.

Negotiations for new agreements are to begin this autumn. "The biggest question," says Tom McGrath, industrial director of the Irish Congress of Trade Unions, "is if there will be a national agreement at all." The unions want a price control policy that will protect their wage gains, and they want increases in pensions and other fringe benefits. They also want equal wages for women. There is irritation, too, about the tax exemptions for farmers.

The unions win general praise for their reasonableness and their recognition that Ireland must export without interruption to thrive. Strikes are few. "We've had labor peace," says a government official.

Foreign Industry

Masterminding a key segment of the government effort is the Industrial Development Authority, the highly organized group that woos foreign industry to set up installations in Ireland.

It has been notably successful. Between 1960 and the middle of last year, 688 projects were begun in Ireland. About 40 percent were British, 25 percent American, 20 percent German and 5 percent Dutch. Now the Japanese are coming, too.

A recent survey by the US Chamber of Commerce in Ireland put total US investment here at about $410 million and said it had created 17,000 jobs, all but 500 of them held by Irish people.

That suits the Industrial Development Authority fine. "Our basic aim is to create jobs for workers," says George O'Hara, an official of the authority. The authority figures it has created 60,000 jobs since 1960, and it now aims to create 15,000 a year.

DENMARK'S SUPPORT WAVERS [4]

The British call for renegotiation has stimulated the already lively Danish opposition against the EEC and triggered off the idea of holding a second Danish referendum on membership if the British actually withdraw. In an effort to stem the withdrawal tide the foreign minister, Mr. Ove

[4] From "Then There Were Seven?" *Economist* (London). 251:66. Ap. 20, '74. Reprinted by permission.

Guldberg, who is a keen community supporter, has declared
categorically that there would be no reason for Denmark to
leave if Britain quit the EEC. And this was later repeated
to the parliamentary committee on EEC affairs. For Mr.
Guldberg, the prospect of losing the EEC's huge farm sub-
sidy and devaluing the krone by 30 percent or more is an
alarming one.

But Mr. Guldberg is not a free agent. The minority government . . . has only 22 seats out of 179, and the influence
of the all-party parliamentary committee on the EEC will
be paramount. . . .

The new EEC debate in Denmark has deeply annoyed
the business community as well as the government and
moderate Social Democrats. As in Britain, bad economic
policy and bad luck are blamed on the Common Market.
The latest opinion polls show as many people against membership as for it, with a substantial proportion of don't-
knows who might come out against the EEC if Britain were
to withdraw.

CAP: "P" IS FOR PROBLEMS [5]

The Common Agricultural Policy represents the major
adjustment for the new members. The community formulated the policy in a series of lengthy negotiations in the
late sixties to further its goal of a single market in which
not only industrial goods but all goods, people, business and
capital can move freely. The aim was to set common price
levels for farm products so that they could circulate without
restrictions among the members; to replace the various national subsidies for agriculture with a uniform system of
guaranteed prices; and to provide increased protection for
community farmers from lower-priced imports from third
countries.

[5] From *Great Decisions 1973*. Topic No. 5: "The Common Market Expands:
Can the U.S. Compete?" Foreign Policy Association. 345 E. 46th St. New York
10017. '73. p 51-2. Reprinted with permission from *Great Decisions 1973*. Copyright
1973 by the Foreign Policy Association, Inc.

The protectionist feature of the Common Agricultural Policy was incorporated primarily for social and political reasons. Some 13 percent of the six founding members' labor force earn their living farming. Although their numbers are declining (in 1960 they represented 21 percent of the labor force), farmers continue to exercise political influence disproportionate to their share of the vote. A majority have small holdings—too small to be very profitable. Of six million farms in the community (pre-enlargement), 80 percent are under thirty acres. Only two farmers out of ten make a decent living; the rest earn a third less than the average industrial worker.

If the smaller producers had to lower their prices enough to compete against imports, they would be wiped out. Even with subsidies, life on the farm is difficult enough. The suicide rate among French farmers far exceeds the rate in any other segment of the population. And in Belgium, one out of four producers owning less than twenty-five acres is unmarried.

High Prices, Huge Surpluses

The Common Agricultural Policy was intended to provide owners of small- and medium-sized farms with an adequate standard of living—adequate, that is, to live on but not so generous that it would discourage marginal producers from eventually leaving the land. In this respect, and in others, the Common Agricultural Policy fell short of the mark. Even its architect, Dr. Sicco L. Mansholt of the Netherlands, has had to admit that it had flaws.

The owners of small- and medium-sized farms were unhappy because the guaranteed minimum prices were too low to enable them to make ends meet. The same prices, however, often provided a windfall for the largest, most efficient farmers, who overproduced and in the process reaped sizable profits. In high-production years, this left governments with enormous surpluses to dispose of either by stockpiling—which meant costly storage charges—or by dumping overseas at less than cost. The six in 1969 accumulated so much butter that the surplus weighed nearly as much as Austria's entire population. . . .

Although a common market in agricultural goods is closer to realization today than ever before, there are still some obstacles to the free flow of produce across borders. Dutch margarine, for example, sold in the Netherlands, must be identified as margarine on the package and must be enriched with vitamins. But Dutch margarine cannot be sold in Belgium if it contains vitamins. And although the package does not need to be labeled, it must be cube-shaped to meet Belgian law.

Farm Subsidy Fund

For the new members, Britain in particular, the largest net importer of food in the world, the agricultural policy poses problems. Food prices are rising to conform to the community's common price level. And British food imports from third countries (exceptions were made in the case of British dairy imports from New Zealand and sugar from the West Indies) are subject to the variable levy [see Glossary]. Revenue from the levy is paid into the community's central farm fund, which is used to support guaranteed minimum prices, to help the neediest farmers improve their production and to subsidize the export of surpluses.

EUROPE'S FARM MUDDLE[6]

From the shepherds of the Faeroes to the orange pickers of Sicily, there are 10 million farmers—big and small, filthy rich and dirt poor—within the European Common Market. All of them, as well as the other 245 million citizens of the Common Market (or European Economic Community) live under a protectionist and increasingly creaky farm system

[6] From article by Richard C. Longworth, European diplomatic correspondent for United Press International. *Saturday Review/World.* 1:12-15. O. 9, '73. Reprinted by permission.

that is almost certain to strain relations between Europe and the United States.

The system, framed eleven years ago, is called the Common Agricultural Policy (CAP). Its purpose was to give Europeans plenty of food at reasonable prices while raising the income of European farmers—many no more than peasants—to the level of industrial workers. Today it ranks, along with the Common Market's customs union, as one of the only two pillars constructed so far in the much-proclaimed edifice of European unity.

Yet by most yardsticks CAP is a failure. Farm incomes lag hopelessly behind those in town, while food prices are among the world's highest. There are signs that CAP is beginning to choke on its own red tape. And the system has displayed a vulnerability to both nonsense and fraud. . . .

The Common Agricultural Policy was written into the 1958 Treaty of Rome for the same reason that a customs union was included for industrial goods: The Common Market, to be realistic, had to include food. But while the customs union quickly began to reduce tariffs between the original six Common Market members, it took five years to get CAP moving—a portent of the hairsplitting and compromises that have followed.

CAP is based on two props, and they have caused most of its problems. The first is external tariffs. One basic tariff sets fixed duties on such items as wine, fruit, and vegetables; it is not necessarily crippling to importers. But there is another tariff wall—the infamous "variable levy." Think of a crossbar that is always just a bit higher than an athlete can jump, and you have an idea of the variable levy. It is called variable because it goes up and down from week to week, reflecting price changes in such key commodities as grain and milk. Its purpose is to keep the price of imports always a fraction higher than that of local produce. If an American grain costs $2.00 per bushel while the same grain grown in Europe costs $3.00, then the levy will be set at something like $1.10 per bushel, raising the price of the US grain to $3.10 and giving European farmers a constant, unbeatable edge.

Having blocked competition from outside, CAP prevents it at home with its second prop. This prop is a combination of price supports based on guaranteed prices and subsidies for exports. The latter are necessary because high-cost European farm output could not compete abroad at European prices. When most European produce is sold abroad, therefore, its price falls and the farmer gets the difference in direct subsidies from a giant Common Market kitty called the European Agricultural Guidance and Guarantee Fund, which doles out some $4.5 billion per year—two thirds of the total EEC budget.

It does not take an economist to predict the result of such a system. With this much protection of inefficiency, European farmers have no need to be efficient. One result is high supermarket prices that cut even further into European family budgets than they would into higher American incomes. Wholesale prices average 65 percent above world prices, and European consumer costs can only amaze an American housewife who joins a boycott rather than pay $2.00 a pound for steak. My local Brussels supermarket, for instance, is charging $3.63 per pound for the equivalent of a T-bone, $1.24 for a dozen eggs, $1.57 for a pound of butter. Chicken is $1.08 per pound. These are normal prices, brought on not by shortages but often by surpluses.

CAP's natural bent toward foolishness surfaced . . . [in 1973] in the case of Russia and the butter mountain. With a guaranteed price of $1.13 per pound for butter and with competition locked out by that tariff wall, European dairy farmers produce yearly more butter than shoppers can buy. Under CAP rules the Common Market must buy up this surplus and store it on the "butter mountain"—actually, several warehouses scattered around Europe. By early 1973 the mountain amounted to 400,000 tons. European taxpayers had paid some $855 million to buy the stuff from farmers, not counting storage fees.

At this point, the Soviet government proposed to buy up half the mountain—200,000 tons—to meet a Russian butter shortage. But the Soviets offered only 19 cents per pound—one sixth of what it cost the Common Market in the first place and one eighth of what a European pays in the store. The offer was greeted indignantly by the newspapers and parliaments of Europe. But the Common Market accepted it. Officials explained that the butter, if dumped on markets, would undercut existing prices and ruin farmers. A small amount goes to pensioners and to dependents of soldiers, but this barely dents the mountain. In short, the cut-rate sale to Russia was the most economical solution available. Within a fortnight Soviet ships arrived in Antwerp to load it aboard.

Three months later Pierre Lardinois, the Common Market commissioner for agriculture, reported that the Russian sale had had about the same effect on the butter mountain that a brisk war has on the population explosion. The CAP butter surplus, he said, had already climbed back to 350,000 tons and would be well above 400,000 tons by the end of the year.

The subsidies CAP gives for food exports and the casual way in which the exports are policed provide a fertile field for fraud. In one case four men—two Frenchmen, a West German, and a Belgian—collected export rebates for French wheat that they said was going outside the Common Market. Instead, it was going next door to Germany, where it was sold at the high CAP-guaranteed prices. These men were caught, but critics in European parliaments say that other swindlers are taking the EEC for an undetected $125 million per year. Common Market leaders say this is "grossly exaggerated," but the truth is that no one really knows. The Common Market, having no police or customs inspectors of its own, must rely on help from the bureaucracies of its nine members and on an auditing system totally unable to cope with the smoother forms of fraud.

CAP's price-fixing apparatus is so elaborate that EEC

headquarters in Brussels must make seventy separate calculations each week for each of three hundred products on which it sets a price. During the recent monetary upheavals, the EEC sent out a Telex message eighty-one feet long just to list new tariffs on food imports. The *Financial Times* of London has proclaimed CAP to be "simply unworkable," and West German Agricultural Minister Josef Ertl calls it "idiotic."

The red tape is complicated by the fact that all CAP calculations are made in "units of account," a make-believe currency, and then are translated into the nine different currencies of the member nations. The unit of account was invented to help CAP keep farm prices equal in all nine nations. This means it should have a constant value in all nine. But recent currency changes, such as the repeated revaluations of the Deutsche Mark, have thrown all calculations on equal prices askew. This has led CAP officials to formulate a complicated set of special levies and taxes in order to equalize things again. But with six Common Market currencies floating together and three others floating separately, with Germany revaluing periodically and Denmark contemplating devaluation, and with the US dollar off on a drunken trajectory of its own, these levies and taxes pile one on top of another. The compensatory taxes, when first introduced, were meant to be temporary. But West German farmers, who became their main beneficiaries, like most recipients of a windfall, hate to let them go. West Germany's Ertl, who owes his seat in the Bundestag [lower house of parliament] to the Bavarian farm vote, once walked out of a Common Market meeting rather than agree to dismantle the tax structure.

Thus far, certainly, little of the money paid in high market prices has filtered down to the farmers, with the exception of big growers in France and Holland. Of the subsidies and supports flowing from the CAP budget, fully 80 percent goes to only one third of Europe's farmers. Italian farmers, after eleven years of CAP, remain poor. Large pockets of rural poverty persist in Germany and parts of France. . . . Dutch farmers earn, on the average, nearly three times as much as Irish ones. The average European farmer, even today, owns about twenty-five acres and barely makes ends meet.

The reason, basically, is that there are too many farmers working too small farms. Europeans, like Americans, have found that, in farming, bigness equals prosperity. With the high investment that farming requires, even CAP's price supports have . . . [only] kept small farmers struggling along on a marginal basis. Much of the money is siphoned off by middlemen before it reaches the farm. And only the biggest farmers, particularly wheat growers, are geared to take advantage of the real CAP bounty—export subsidies. The rest produce for local markets.

Thus some large European wheat farmers are millionaires. More typical are the hundreds of thousands of small herdsmen nurturing their cattle for two thousand dollars a year or less. Many have given up. . . .

The EEC, realizing that its farms are overpopulated, belatedly made the exodus from the farm an official policy and adopted a ten-year plan to keep the trend going. The program is called the Mansholt Plan, after Dr. Sicco Mansholt, the Dutchman who retired . . . [in 1973] after fourteen years as the EEC agricultural commissioner and six months as its president. The plan aims at cutting the Common Market's current farm population by half (to five million in 1980), by training young marginal farmers for industry and pensioning off older farmers. Other features include soil banks to avoid surpluses, encouragement of meat production, discouragement of dairy gluts, and modernization of the farms that are left when the migration ends. The eventual aim is larger farms and higher technology, on the American model.

It took Mansholt four years to get his plan approved by the EEC's member nations. It was to have gone into effect last year but has been postponed until next year, and few observers believe it will start then. The target date of 1980 probably is a pipe dream. Meanwhile, because of natural causes, the European farm population continues to shrink by 3 to 4 percent per year.

Why the resistance to change? One reason is CAP's status as one of the few real Common Market accomplishments so far. Its tangible manifestations, good or bad, have instilled an inordinate pride in some defenders of European unity, who fear that any reform of existing institutions will jeopardize future progress. More important is CAP's original concept, which was less an economic outline than a social policy. Its supporters have always seen it as a ladder bringing farmers up from poverty and into the prosperity of postwar Europe. Only on this basis can its soak-the-consumer aspects be justified. Belief in CAP now depends more on faith than on facts, but this is not so important. What counts is the blind reverence it inspires in many sectors of the Common Market. Within these sectors criticism is heresy.

Sometimes this support is not so blind. Large-scale French farmers have done very well out of CAP. They are politically powerful, and the French government has rejected any tampering with the structure that has brought them so many benefits. Thus prospects for real progress appear slim, unless CAP's critics can marshal the growing discontent of the harried consumers.

But appearances could deceive. For CAP has never been without its critics, and these critics are more numerous today. They can count on widespread, if unorganized, support from consumers. And, for the first time, they have breached both the bureaucracy and the farming establishment. . . .

EEC commissioner Altiero Spinelli has been campaigning for Europe to "end its excessive dependence on high prices to guarantee farm incomes." Spinelli would freeze farm prices and limit the amount of surpluses that the Common Market would automatically purchase. There may be a transatlantic trade war, he warns, unless Europe "man-

ages to curb the powerful sugar and cereals lobbies and re-
stores agricultural prices to their role of market regulators,
discarding its ultraprotectionist attitude on these products."
Spinelli has now won important support from Sir Christopher Soames, son-in-law of Sir Winston Churchill and the
man in charge of leading Europe into the Nixon Round
[the seventh postwar round of trade negotiations]. As the
EEC commissioner for external affairs, Soames is in a better
position than Spinelli to affect policy. CAP is highly un-
popular in Britain; and within the EEC bureaucracy there
are joking predictions that if Soames can change the European farm picture, a peerage for him is assured. Soames
has one big advantage: He used to be British ambassador to
Paris and is an old hand at dealing with the French.

The most discussed prospective reform is the use of
subsidies and deficiency payments—straightforward government handouts to farmers to enable them to sell their products at lower prices. This idea has no place in the Mansholt
Plan. But Britain has used a similar method at home and
is pushing it now in Europe.

A potential major challenge to CAP is brewing in Germany, where an advisory committee to the agricultural ministry has recommended that Germany drop out of the common price-fixing system and set food costs on a national
basis. The committee said Germany should stick with the
rest of CAP's policies, such as the variable levy system. But
its price recommendation, if adopted by the government,
would be such a breach in European agricultural unity that
the entire CAP would begin to unravel.

Other European voices are also beginning to assail CAP,
which the *Times* of London has called a "costly and socially
regressive failure." But perhaps the loudest thunder comes
from the United States, where the government has said it
wants . . . to open up European markets to American farm
exports—unlike the Kennedy Round, which cut industrial
tariffs but had little liberalizing effect on food trade. Secretary of Agriculture Earl L. Butz told a meeting in Paris that

"we do not understand how it can happen that a market as wealthy as Europe should not be open to American produce. For what reasons should the European system of protection be considered sacrosanct?" This sort of blunt talk, while true enough, puts CAP's defenders on guard against any change . . . and defeats the efforts of those, like Soames, who would modify it slowly. . . .

The best American strategy would seem to be to avoid frontal assaults on CAP and instead make quiet common cause with the many Europeans who feel it is time to drop excessive protectionism and try something new. Spinelli and Soames can count on a growing cadre of followers, particularly in Britain and Germany. During a review of CAP scheduled for later this year, the Common Market will consider "structural reforms." France is highly suspicious of this and in normal times would veto any reforms. But these are not normal times. Both the world food picture and trade relations are changing fast. Powerful forces seek to remake Europe's agricultural dinosaur. If Americans trumpet their desire to destroy CAP, these forces will have no choice but to rally to its defense. But American pressures applied subtly on the side of the angels could bring a billion-dollar advantage to American exporters—and at the same time do a favor for long-suffering European shoppers.

TALE OF THREE COUNTRIES [7]

In terms of real economic growth, 1973 was one of the best years on record for the industrialized nations of the world. Their economies grew by more than 6 percent overall, because production hit high levels in a good many of these nations at the same time. The year's remarkable economic growth was accompanied, however, by accelerating inflation, fast-climbing interest rates, and international monetary strains. And, of course, toward the end of the year

[7] From "A Bad Year for the Rich Countries," by Lawrence A. Mayer, member, board of editors. *Fortune*. 90:158+. Ag. '74. Reprinted by permission.

came the damaging effects of oppressive increases in the price of crude oil.

As a result, 1974 is proving to be an exceptionally unpleasant year for the richer nations of the world. We have the problems of 1973, and others besides, without the consolations of vigorous growth. It now appears that the overall growth rate for the developed world will not even reach 2 percent this year, the lowest in sixteen years. And 1975 may not be much better.

Signs of financial distress, public as well as private, are already evident. The city of Rome has suspended interest payments on its massive debts, and the creditworthiness of the Italian national government has been questioned. With interest rates high and stock prices low throughout the world, a great many companies are finding it exceedingly expensive to raise capital—in some cases, prohibitively so.

A number of individual banks have run into trouble. They include Franklin National in the United States and Herstatt in Germany, as well as lesser institutions in Italy, Britain, and elsewhere. In an unusual effort to maintain confidence in the international banking system, the central bankers of major countries have let word be spread that within their own countries they will assist banks threatened by the general liquidity squeeze. . . .

Besides intensifying inflation around the world, the quadrupling of oil prices has created grave problems in international trade and finance. Most advanced nations will be running deficits this year on their current accounts (mainly international trade in goods and services). Primarily because of the immense increase in payments for oil imports, the combined deficit of the advanced nations may run to $40 billion. . . .

Italy

Italy's economy is fragile. During most of the 1960s its growth rate was enviably robust, but beginning with a wave of strikes in late 1969, Italy frittered away a chance to become a first-rank economy. Over the years, weak and unstable governments became a drag on economic progress. They created a class of "golden bureaucrats"—civil servants with high pensions—and allowed an enormous number of other people to feed at the public trough.

The country was especially hard hit by the higher costs of oil and other commodities, since to a large extent its economy is based on the transformation of imported raw materials into manufactured goods for export. By last spring Italy was in such a state that Guido Carli, the forceful governor of its central bank, issued a stern warning: "Today's problem is not that of the quality of life in the factory, but that of the continuing life of the factory."

In May, the country moved to curb imports of consumer goods, including the expensive beef that Italians—to the horror of some economists—had grown very fond of. Stringent limits were also put on bank credit, and the country borrowed heavily abroad to help meet its external deficit. But all of this added up to just a stopgap program. And it didn't stop the gap very effectively—for example, the French were able to keep their beef flowing into Italy by supplying credit to Italian importers.

. . . [In July 1974], after much internal dissension, the political parties, trade unions, and big corporations got together, more or less, on an ambitious program to put Italy on the path to solvency. Tariffs were raised sharply. Taxes were increased on luxury goods, and efforts to tighten up the inefficient tax-collection process were promised. These and other measures should serve to reduce the budget deficit and cut excess imports. Capital stashed abroad is already on its way home—a cheering bit of news. There has been some relaxation of limits on bank credit for small enterprises, both to help them survive and to maintain employment.

Bruno Brovedani, chief economist of the Banca Nazionale del Lavoro, thinks that Italy's GNP will increase about 4.5 percent in real terms for the year as a whole. But he expects the new program to cool off the economy toward the end of this year and into 1975.

The labor unions are already sponsoring sporadic strikes to protest some of the tough new policies, but those policies please Italian businessmen, by and large. Says Umberto Agnelli, the managing director of Fiat: "For the short term I'm pessimistic, for the medium and long term, I'm optimistic." In spite of Italy's problems, he believes that his country has "a very great strength." . . .

France

France is making a fresh attack on some long-standing problems under the leadership of its new president, Valéry Giscard d'Estaing. An economic expert, Giscard aims to give French workers a better deal; up to now, they have benefited less from national economic growth than workers in most of the other West European countries. Giscard has raised pensions, minimum wages, and family allowances. He is seeking guarantees of a year's pay for workers who lose jobs because of economic conditions.

The government plans to raise income taxes, principally of corporations and high-income individuals. Taxes on fuels also are going up. Consumer spending is being discouraged by tighter credit, and interest rates on savings accounts have been raised. Controls will be imposed on the use of heating oil.

All of these measures are intended to keep the budget in trim, while cutting France's bill for imported oil and freeing more goods for export. Meanwhile, an existing ceiling on increases in total bank credit is being more strictly enforced, and the central bank's discount rate has been pushed to 13 percent, the highest in the industrialized world. Giscard is trying to get the French inflation rate—now about 13 percent—down to 7 percent in 1975.

Another of Giscard's important moves involves a big deal with Iran. In the next decade, France is to help that country with a lot of advanced-technology projects, including nuclear power plants and a subway system for Teheran. This deal, valued at $4 billion, will partially offset France's oil bill. But the transaction blocks other countries from the possibility of meeting *their* oil deficits by selling to Iran. And in going to grand-scale barter, France is turning the economic clock back. Says one French economist: "For three centuries the path of progress has been to get away from barter to the use of money as an intermediary. Bartering is characteristic of the propensity of states to interfere in trade."

West Germany

West Germany remains the strongest economy in Europe. With the continent's stiffest monetary and fiscal policies, it has held the inflation rate to about 7 percent—even though wage increases have been running to 12 and even 14 percent. As a consequence, profit margins have been squeezed.

Restrictive governmental policies slowed the growth rate in the first half of the year, and growth for the year as a whole may be no more than 2.5 percent. Unemployment is rising, largely because industries such as autos, construction, and textiles are having a poor year, and the government—astonishingly for inflation-shy Germany—is contemplating a tax cut for 1975 as a tonic for the economy.

The big export industries—steel and machinery especially—continue to do amazingly well despite the revaluations of the Mark. The conventional explanation for this sturdy performance cites the quality, reliability, and quick delivery of German goods. But Britain's three-day workweek earlier this year helped by bringing a switch of orders to West German manufacturers.

West Germany exports so much of its production that a good deal of the benefits from its gains in GNP go abroad. Otto von Fieandt of the Paris-based firm of economic consultants, Eurofinance, calculates that the increase in the standard of living of West Germans last year lagged about two percentage points behind the increase in total GNP.

West Germany holds two important cards in the world oil game. First, its total exports exceed imports by a large margin, even counting in oil. This makes Germany a large potential lender to oil-deficit countries. The other card is an abundance of coal. Until recently a good many mines were uneconomic, but the new high price of oil has improved the arithmetic of coal.

Getting coal production to much higher levels will require large investments, however, and so will the development of coal-gasification technology. Germany produced gasoline out of coal in World War II, but the process is relatively expensive—gasoline from coal costs more than gasoline from crude oil, even today. Exactly how West Germany exploits its coal reserves will depend to a considerable degree on what energy-sharing policies emerge in the European Community [EC]—and what happens to oil prices.

THE ENERGY MARKET [8]

Electric lights would not light, cars could not be driven, and a hot cup of coffee would be hard to come by without energy. Energy in one form or another lights streets, heats homes, and constructs planes, factories, and footballs. It is the consumer society's most consumed commodity.

In 1970, the nine . . . [European Community] members needed the equivalent of 1.2 billion tons of coal to supply energy for homes, cars, and industries. They had little trouble providing it. In the past, energy was among the least of Europe's worries. The original six members of the community had their own coal supply in the mines of Germany, France, Belgium, and the Netherlands; natural gas was relatively abundant within community borders; and, above all, there was a seemingly limitless flow of oil from the Middle East's enormous reserves.

The worldwide economics of energy tended to keep that

[8] From "Power: Society's Most Consumed Product," by John Nielsen, an American journalist working in Brussels. *European Community*. 164:8-11. Ap. '73.

situation stable. Traditionally self-sufficient in oil, the United States maintained a system of import quotas that, in effect, turned the world's oil toward Europe where no such restrictions existed. Today, it seems, everyone worries about energy supplies. The United States, no longer self-sufficient, currently imports fully 20 percent of its oil requirements, and some estimates put its imports in 1980 at about the same level as Europe's total current consumption. Japan, too, has become a major importer of oil.

World demand has risen alarmingly in recent years and so have oil prices. [In 1974 the price of oil quadrupled.— Ed.] The oil-producing nations have . . . demonstrated a new ability to bargain effectively for higher prices. Moreover, the chronically unstable Middle East, which holds more than half the world's known reserves, could for political reasons shut off oil supplies at any time—a fact demonstrated to the community during the 1956 Suez Canal crisis. [It was demonstrated again in the October 1973 Mideast war.—Ed.]

Energy has become a seller's market, and the community cannot afford to depend upon one main source for its oil supplies. Meanwhile, demand continues to grow, and the community must take steps to guarantee that it will find supplies to meet it. Against this international backdrop, the community leaders at the Paris summit last October [1972] charged the community institutions with drawing up a common energy policy "as soon as possible."

EC's Energy Market Fragmented in Early Days

The summit, however, was hardly the beginning. The six had been groping toward a common energy policy for years but were hampered by several factors. First, none of the community treaties provides for a common energy policy. In fact, their very nature militates against centralization and coordination by dividing responsibility for the different energy sectors. Coal is the province of the European Coal and Steel Community (ECSC), established in 1952.

Atomic energy rests with the European Atomic Energy Community (Euratom), established in 1958. Everything else, including oil, natural gas, electricity, and hydroelectric power, comes under the 1958 European Economic Community (EEC) treaty.

The situation reflects the times in which the treaties were drafted. Coal, an indigenous resource, was Europe's dominant energy source, accounting for 75 percent of total consumption in 1950 compared to 10 percent for oil. During the early sixties, however, the community's coal industry declined rapidly in the face of competition from low-priced foreign imports, primarily from the United States. By 1966, coal accounted for only 38 percent of the community's energy consumption, while oil provided 45 percent. Despite a growing demand for energy, coal production actually fell. National authorities then established a variety of national support systems which fragmented the community's energy market.

The Paris Treaty, founding document of the ECSC, bans coal subsidies but does not provide for a common external tariff on coal. The member states were free either to protect their own industries by raising external tariffs or to import at world prices. The different degrees to which they did one or the other led to varying energy costs within the six, with the advantage going to those countries with small or no coal industries and easy access to low-priced imports.

Uneven competition in energy led to distortion in other sectors because energy makes up a significant portion of the total cost of most industrial goods—26 percent in steel, 16 percent in chemicals, 15 percent in nonferrous metals, for example.

The first step toward solving these problems, and thus toward a common energy policy, came in 1964 when the Council of Ministers adopted an ECSC–proposed protocol of agreement calling for cheap and secure energy supplies, fair competition among the various sources of energy, and freedom of choice for the consumer. Because coal's decline posed potentially severe regional problems, the protocol also called for coordination of state subsidies to that industry. Coal thus became an exception to the Paris Treaty, which bans subsidies under normal conditions, and the community set a course toward a low-price energy policy.

The next initiative came in 1968 when the Commission published a memorandum to the council entitled "First Guidelines for a Common Energy Policy." A detailed and comprehensive document, it addressed itself to the entire energy spectrum. . . .

The Commission took a second major initiative in October 1972, when it submitted a series of documents for review and approval by the council. Included in the package were . . . two documents [which] update the "first guidelines" and take into account changes in the world energy market since 1970 and the increased importance now attached to environmental protection.

Energy Demand Growing

Between now and 1985, world demand for energy will grow at an annual rate of about 6 percent, and total yearly consumption will more than double. Although the community's rate of demand growth will be below the average (at just over 5 percent), the nine will need the equivalent of 2.3 billion tons of coal by 1985, most of which will have to be imported. About 60 percent of total oil consumed will have to be imported . . .

The need for enormous investments in exploration and equipment is an inevitable result of diversifying the community's supply sources. Most of the easily reached, inexpensively exploited reserves in the world are already known, and new sources must be sought in such difficult or out-of-the-way places as seabeds or Alaska's North Shelf. The North Sea, made economically feasible by rising oil costs, is an important plus for the community. Most of its resources will be consumed in Britain, but it will contribute significantly to reducing the community's dependence on Middle East oil.

To ensure maximum exploitation of the North Sea, the Commission proposes a common information program on oil exploration and exploitation with emphasis on the continental shelf. To hedge against crisis, the Commission has also recommended the community's oil stockpile be gradually increased to 120 days' supply.

Natural Gas as an Alternative

Among the currently available alternatives to oil, natural gas would seem at first glance to offer the best short-term advantages. It is cheaper than oil, although its price is generally pegged to petroleum products and will rise during the coming decade. The community has significant natural gas reserves within its own borders and territorial waters, primarily in the Netherlands and the North Sea. Moreover, natural gas is the cleanest of the hydrocarbon fuels, a decided advantage in a pollution-conscious, highly industrialized society. . . .

Coal is a theoretically viable alternative to oil in many applications, but the level of foreign coal imports is governed more by economic and social considerations than by demand for energy. The domestic coal industry's production costs are too high to allow it to compete on a worldwide basis. Nonetheless, the mines must be kept open because they are an ultimate safety valve in the event of a serious energy crisis [e.g., the oil crisis of 1973–1974] and because closing them would cause serious unemployment and regional problems. At present, community mines are the principal source of coking coal for the community's iron industry . . . .

Nuclear Energy Holds the Key

The brightest hope for the future lies with the atom. Its use as an energy source would have an advantageous impact on the entire energy market . . .

The community, however, must wait years before nuclear industry will be economically viable on a large scale. Nuclear activity in the community is dispersed among too many marginally profitable, essentially isolated firms. Moreover, investment costs in the early stages of conversion are still prohibitive, even though nuclear energy itself is cheap. Investment costs can be lowered in the long run, only by a high level of equipment standardization and volume production not yet achieved in Europe. . . .

Electricity is not strictly speaking a primary energy source, but its importance to the community's total economy gives it a special place in any common energy policy. The Commission hopes to consolidate and harmonize the community's electricity markets to allow creation of larger central power stations. Ideally, the community will someday be supplied by a rationally designed network of stations providing for the most economical distribution of electricity, without regard to national boundaries.

A COMMON ENERGY POLICY? [9]

Last winter's energy crisis made development of a common energy policy by the European Community more urgent and less likely. When the Arabs raised oil prices, cut production, and placed a total oil embargo on the Netherlands and a partial embargo on Denmark, the other member countries of the community each, in effect, opted for a national rather than a community approach to the problem. Since the darkest days of the winter, some progress has been made toward what the Europeans call a "global" energy policy, but that progress has been slow. And while the Europeans appear to be much closer to cooperating on a significant energy R & D [research and development] program and exchange of relevant information, they still seem

[9] From "European Community Energy Policy: Regulation or Mainly Information?" by John Walsh, head, news staff. *Science.* 184:1158-61. Je. 14, '74. Copyright 1974 by the American Association for the Advancement of Science. Reprinted by permission.

very far from agreement on any effective plan to deal in a united way with the oil companies or the oil-producing countries.

On one energy question of increasing importance—uranium enrichment—the energy crisis does seem to have hastened the community toward decisive action. But just as the debate on uranium enrichment has centered on when and by what means the Europeans should end their heavy dependence on United States nuclear fuel enrichment capacity, the forging of a comprehensive energy policy involves complex questions of relations with other countries, notably the United States and the Middle Eastern oil-producing countries.

Answers Coming

Some of the Europeans' foot-dragging on formulating an energy policy can be ascribed to questions of the extent to which community countries can expect to share American fossil-fuel supplies—particularly coal—and to cooperate in energy R & D programs. . . .

Even without the problems of external relations, internal difficulties have been serious enough to impede progress toward a community energy policy. One of the stickiest issues remaining is the role of the oil companies, particularly of the "majors" such as BP (British Petroleum) and Shell. A main aim of the community energy group is to obtain greater "transparency" in the workings of the companies in order that the community can make informed policy decisions. Brussels officials are seeking to increase the checks on company operations, but, as in the United States, this is proving no simple task. Adoption of a community energy policy will require the approval by the council— the community's top authority—of recommendations made by the Commission. The commissioners are appointed by the member countries but are expected to put forward proposals which embody a community solution, and they generally do. The council is comprised of ministerial-level representatives of the member governments, and its members are actuated much more directly by national interests. The Commission has put forward a detailed proposal on energy policy but has so far failed to persuade the council to approve it. . . .

The Commission effort to formulate an energy policy was ordered in a summit meeting of community prime ministers held in the cold gray light of the energy crisis in December [1973] in Copenhagen. In an apparent effort to cover all bets, the prime ministers told the commissioners to come up with a common energy policy which provided machinery for rapid decision making, allowed for wide-scale cooperation with oil-producing countries, and helped secure stable energy supplies at reasonable prices.

The community initiative on energy policy has been carried by an energy committee headed by Henri Simonet, a Belgian-appointed vice president of the Commission, who is mainly responsible for energy affairs in the Brussels executive. Since the beginning of . . . [1974] several proposals on energy have gone to the council—one on stockpiling fuel for power plants and another for a system of price monitoring of petroleum products, for example. . . .

European Project Independence

The Simonet proposals apparently resemble the US Project Independence in recommending medium-term (to 1985) measures and long-term (to 2000) measures and in contemplating at least a degree of energy independence for Europe. Reportedly, the proposals call for energy conservation and for rationalization of the use of various kinds of energy. . . .

Probably most controversial is a proposal for a community energy agency. Such an agency would apparently have responsibility for developing existing and new community energy resources and would be expected to construct the infrastructure required to carry on community energy research and technology development. The agency would also be at least partly responsible for storage of fuels and for security of fuel supplies.

There are plenty of potential points of friction in the proposals. The French, for example, reportedly were astonished and pained by the proposal to keep the level of coal production in the community at 240 million tons a year—minable coal reserves in Western Europe are virtually all in Britain and West Germany, and cost of coal research and production could be high.

Reservations about an energy agency are doubtless reinforced by experience with Euratom, the European atomic energy agency. Ironically, Euratom was in part a product of an energy crisis that did not occur. The Suez war of 1956 seemed to raise the threat of reduced supplies and higher prices of oil. The threat did not really materialize, but the post-Suez atmosphere encouraged the six member countries of the Common Market to collaborate in developing nuclear energy for peaceful purposes.

Euratom

Euratom's poor track record is generally attributed to the unwillingness of the community's member nations—particularly France and Germany—to sacrifice the interests of their own national nuclear industries to a community effort. Other factors contributed. Euratom scientists were granted civil service status from the start, and many used their job security to pursue their own specialized scientific interests, in some cases not very hard. There were individual exceptions, of course, and some good work was done. But, in general, the Euratom staff "lost their scientific reputation," as one Brussels official put it, and came to be regarded "like museum guards."

Disenchantment with Euratom by 1968 was strong enough to cause the discontinuance of multiyear budgets and the start of five years of grudging, annual budgets which made continuity in the agency's program impossible. Euratom research is carried out in four laboratories—at

Ispra in Italy, Geel in Belgium, Karlsruhe in Germany, and Petten in the Netherlands. Of these four labs, which comprise the agency's Joint Research Centre, Ispra is the largest and was reputed to be most notably in decline.

Part of Euratom's problem was that, while other useful areas of research might beckon—environmental research, for example—the agency's latitude in broadening its program was severely limited by the Euratom treaty and, later, by the agency's lackluster reputation.

Finally, last year the newly enlarged community moved to deal with the Euratom problem. A four-year budget was granted on the understanding that the agency would be roundly reorganized. In fact, several hundred people have been separated from the Joint Research Centre's permanent staff of about two thousand in order to make way for recruits from the new member countries and new talent generally. But the purge has been conducted in the polite paternalistic tradition of the community, with most of those departing getting the "golden handshake" (a generous payoff) rather than the unceremonious boot. Euratom is expected to continue solid work in progress on nuclear fusion and hydrogen research and other energy- and environment-related R & D. This will be clearer when a revised program . . . is "finalized."

Some observers trace the difficulties of formulating energy policy for the community to the same source of failure which afflicted Euratom—the protection of national industrial interests. The same issue is reported to be rearing its head in the ECG [the Energy Coordination Group, which grew out of the February 1974 Washington energy conference], with the Europeans finding American companies sticky about discussing certain budding energy technologies. The main issue between the Commission and the council over a community energy policy is said to be a disagreement over the extent to which the community should intervene in the "organization of the market," that is, whether the community should be content with simply eliciting information from energy companies or should take steps to regulate prices and company operations.

To an outsider the rate of community progress toward an energy policy seems hardly to exceed the speed of continental drift. But there is another view by which it might be held remarkable that there is any progress at all. If the energy crisis increased the need for a common energy policy, it also stimulated an opposite and at least equal impulse for member nations to exploit the situation to their national advantage—the French to try to get their money back on the Pierrelatte enrichment plant, Germany to capitalize on its industrial strength, Britain to grow cagier about sharing its bonanza of North Sea oil and natural gas.

The spirit of the community is not the one-for-all-and-all-for-one spirit of *The Three Musketeers*. Experienced community watchers say it is not the acuteness of a problem that makes a member state accept a community solution but the fact that such a solution is more desirable than a national one. They do it because of "their own interest, not the common interest," says one middle-level community official. "Why we have such trouble with the British [is that] they never understand what a community resolve means." The process of compromise and adjustment takes a long time, as in the case of energy policy, and the more senior officials of the community have learned to live with the bureaucratic ballet in Brussels and to tolerate the delays. In considering whether the community is a success or failure they tend to recall the community's accomplishments in trade and to note that, after all, it is no small thing that the community has made it unthinkable that the nations of Western Europe, for the third time in the twentieth century, might again start killing each other by the millions.

WATERSHED FOR THE COMMON MARKET [10]

The year 1973 may still go down as the "Year of Europe," though not for the reasons [Secretary of State] Henry Kissinger had in mind when he christened it that, in his April 23 speech last year. It will be rather that the crises of the past year have made the choices for Europe clearer than ever; they have further shown that if European lack of will and vision led to nothing more serious than division and weakness before, they now are perfectly capable of leading the European Economic Community to disintegration.

In 1973, Europe was indeed, in the words of French Foreign Minister Michel Jobert, "treated like a nonperson" and "humiliated," not only by the United States, Mr. Jobert's favorite target, but by practically everybody. The Soviet Union showed no great solicitude either for France or for the EEC during the year, less than did the United States—unusual considering that in these topsy-turvy days one generally expects better treatment from his adversaries than from his friends. Any relationship Europe may have dreamed of with China was upstaged by Henry Kissinger's ties to Chou En-lai. The Europeans' self-abasement in front of the Arab nations on November 6 [1973], and their approval of a document accepting the Arab interpretations of UN Resolution 242 [of November 1967], did little either for the European reputation or Middle East peace. And it remains to be seen if it earns Europe any special energy privileges in the future. Despite that humiliating gesture, Europe still suffered oil shortages and was obliged to show the world how dependent the once mighty continent was on the tiny sheikdoms of the Persian Gulf. . . .

In all, 1973 was a profoundly humiliating year for the

[10] From "France, the European Crisis and the Alliance," by James O. Goldsborough, chief European correspondent for the *International Herald Tribune*. *Foreign Affairs*. 52:538-44. Ap. '74. Excerpted by permission from *Foreign Affairs*, April 1974. Copyright 1974 by Council on Foreign Relations, Inc.

"world's greatest trading bloc," as it likes to call itself, and then in the new year France was forced to float the franc. In early February the EEC executive Commission judged the situation sufficiently serious to issue an unusual statement in which it pictured Europe in a state of crisis—a "crisis of confidence, a crisis of will and a crisis of lucidity." Despite their wealth, the nine nations were forecasting record deficits and recession resulting from the increased cost of importing reduced quantities of oil, and individual members of the community, particularly Britain and France, were showing their worry by rushing to sign private agreements with whatever oil producer they could, usually in exchange for arms. Even here it appeared that the Europeans would be embarrassed, for in some cases the Arab oil exporters were asking more of them than the Europeans individually were able to supply. . . .

One thing was certain as 1974 got underway, even for those still sanguine about the future of the community: The disruption and increased price of oil supplies from the Middle East had played hell within the European Community just as they did in the whole international community. No one was prepared, and this showed up in the divisive and contradictory actions taken not only by the EEC members, but by other countries that had regarded themselves as allies and judged their international interests to be alike. The cohesion and cooperation of the entire Western world were threatened, and it appeared in the first months of 1974 that efforts both within GATT [General Agreement on Tariffs and Trade] to begin new tariff and trade negotiations during the year and those within the International Monetary Fund to conclude a new monetary agreement would be delayed until order was restored in the oil markets and countries once again could realistically appraise their balance of payments and currency situations.

I think, however, that 1973 will go down as the most significant year for Europe since 1963 (the year of de Gaulle's veto of British EEC membership), and not just because it was the year that Britain finally joined the community. The crises of 1973 provided the strongest evidence yet to the Europeans that they had no hope of maintaining any influence in the world—not enough even to defend their own interests—unless they moved more resolutely toward the political union they have set as their goal for 1980. Far from abandoning that date as some were predicting, not to meet it would be to relegate Europe to the sidelines of history. Outside events resulted in a series of new perceptions on the old continent, even among those members of the Atlantic alliance with closest links to the United States. "In a world whose destiny cannot and should not be determined by two superpowers alone, the influence of a united Europe has become indispensable," West German Chancellor Willy Brandt told the European Parliament in November. This perception of a "condominium," whether in strictly bilateral forums such as the SALT talks [Strategic Arms Limitation Talks], the June 22 agreement, Middle East consultations, trade exchanges, or in the multilateral consultations of mutual and balanced force reductions and the Conference on European Security and Cooperation (where the Europeans "serve as ushers at the US-Soviet marriage," in the words of President Pompidou), contributed greatly to the sense of urgency, if not panic, felt in Europe during the latter part of the year. "Many nations are waiting for [Europe] to show that an alternative [to condominium] exists, and that there are other paths to assure equilibrium in the world," Jobert told a meeting of the Western European Union in November.

Dismiss for a moment the sad spectacle at the year's end, and reflect on what the Europeans achieved politically during 1973. The nine nations caucused and acted together at the Helsinki and Geneva phases of the security conference and coordinated their positions for UN meetings. They sent a single representative to negotiate with the United States on the Atlantic declaration. They spoke with a single voice as the new round of trade talks got underway in Tokyo. In

November, they adopted the notorious Middle East declaration (yes, the Dutch signed that too), which if ineffective in contributing to peace in the area at least showed a common European position and a sense of shared destiny in dealing with the Arabs to assure adequate energy supplies in the future. In December, they held the first of the semiannual summit meetings and produced the document in which they "affirmed their common will to see Europe speak with the same voice in the great affairs of the world." To be sure, some of this momentum was lost during the Washington energy conference where Jobert, in arguing what he thought was the European cause, created division where there had been agreement before, but it still was strong evidence that far from being ready to break up, as some have been predicting, the nine had acquired an embryonic understanding of what is in their own interest. And there still is another argument that pleads strongly in Europe's favor: During 1973 the nine became aware that in many areas they had nobody to turn to but themselves. It was this feeling more than anything else that created difficulties with America when it came to defining future relations.

France, obsessed with superpower domination in a way she had not been since Khrushchev's visit to Camp David almost fifteen years before, was more committed to Europe by the end of 1973 than at any time since 1961 and the first Fouchet Plan draft; West Germany, growing more concerned about US withdrawal and worried over stagnation in her *Ostpolitik*; Britain, coming off a first, tough year of adjustment to life with the continent but showing no signs—even among the Labourites—of throwing in the towel; the smaller EEC countries, relatively tranquil now that Britain was aboard—all of them had a better understanding that, to paraphrase a Kissinger formulation, they were doomed to "creativity together or irrelevance apart."

The difficulties at the year's end and the arguments with the United States over energy and future Atlantic relations only spotlighted the changing relations. "We are still for a

little while longer in this transition phase where the relations between the senior partner, the United States, and the
junior partner, Europe, are transforming themselves into
relations between partners in principle equal," said EEC
Commissioner Ralf Dahrendorf shortly before leaving the
Commission to head the London School of Economics. Dahrendorf's statement showed that much of the difficulty was
precisely the wrenching and tugging going on among the
principal EEC members, and between them and the United
States to define the new relationships. There appeared to be
emerging two quite different conceptions of a united Europe. One of them, pressed by the French, held that the
Atlantic relationship actually impeded the European one.
The French conception, illustrated in part by the European
Community's September draft declaration on Atlantic relations (primarily of British inspiration), stressed Europe's
independence and equality within the alliance, and emphasized that in those areas where Europe still was weak, notably defense, new efforts would be demanded. The other
version, Kissinger's, seemed a new version of the old two-
pillar theory—only this one, like the first one, had a slanting
roof. Moreover, some of the phrases in the US document,
words like "partnership" and "interdependence," were too
strong for the neo-Gaullists (not all of them French), who
preferred notions such as "dialogue" and "independence."

Reconciling these two diverging concepts became the
major exercise of the year and played the dominant role in
creating cross-Atlantic tension. The United States even began complaining about the process being used, for it meant
that each time European and US negotiators got together
the EEC already had a predetermined position, the result of
considerable negotiation among the nine themselves, and
presented the United States with what amounted to a *fait
accompli*. America clearly felt that she had a right to have a
voice in the community's decision-making process. Kissinger
understood the new mood and thought it serious enough to
complain publicly during an end-of-the-year speech to the

Pilgrims in London: "To present the decisions of a unifying Europe to us as *faits accomplis* not subject to effective discussions is alien to the tradition of United States–European relations," he said. Kissinger spelled out in that frank speech what was bothering Washington: The Europeans had "come to believe that their identity should be measured by [their] distance from the United States," he said. And, "Europe's unity must not be at the expense of the Atlantic Community." For the Secretary of State the two notions were completely compatible. In his harshest language he told the Europeans that "in our view, the affirmation of the pervasive nature of our interdependence is not a device for blackmail."

It was left for Jobert to put the difficulties in more colloquial terms:

I suppose that we'll have to complete, sooner or later, a text defining the relations between Europe and the United States because the United States wants one. But it can't be done by saying, "I want this" and "This is the way it is to be." No, no, it will be necessary to be tolerant. When one is among friends, one must put up with one another, accept one another and learn to share. From time to time there will be one who wants to be captain, but the others must say: "It's not your turn anymore."

IV. THE AMERICAN CONNECTION

EDITOR'S INTRODUCTION

Surprisingly, reports *European Community* quoting a Gallup Poll survey, most Americans have never heard of the Common Market. Yet the United States was an early booster of European union, and even though it disagrees with some of the Common Market's policies, it still supports its long-term goals. The state of US relations with the community over the years is reviewed by Boyd France in an excerpt from *A Short Chronicle of United States–European Community Relations*.

In 1973 the United States tried to restore some harmony in its dealings with its old allies. President Nixon declared that 1973 was to be the "Year of Europe," and Secretary of State Kissinger, in an April speech, called for a "new Atlantic Charter." Excerpts from that speech are reprinted in this section. The two declarations had a mixed reception. Some European objections are spelled out by a critic of US policy, former US Ambassador to the European Community J. Robert Schaetzel. The Manchester *Guardian*'s Peter Jenkins throws further light on European reactions.

The future of the Atlantic partnership is the subject of the final selections: a report from the European bureaus of *U.S. News & World Report* and a call for unity by Sir Christopher Soames, a vice president of the European Community Commission.

THE COMMON MARKET, WHAT'S THAT?[1]

Two of every three Americans believe that US ties with Western Europe matter a great deal, while only 16 percent

[1] From "How Americans Rate the European Community." *European Community.* 167:8-9. Jl. '73.

say these ties are not important. *Most Americans (55 percent), however, have never heard of the European Common Market* [European Economic Community or EEC].

These findings are contained in a Gallup Poll released on June 28 [1973] by the European Community Information Service (ECIS) in Washington, D.C. The ECIS commissioned the poll to determine the American public's knowledge of and attitudes toward the European Community [EC]. Gallup based its survey on 1,030 personal interviews, conducted nationwide during the last week of March and in early April, of Americans aged eighteen and older. . . .

Education, income, and sex proved significant variables in the average American's knowledge of the community. The best informed were usually college-educated males with annual incomes of at least fifteen thousand dollars. The most frequently mentioned sources of information about the community were newspapers and magazines. Less than half, 45 percent of all persons interviewed, reported that they had heard or read about the European Community.

An even smaller percentage (35 percent) demonstrated real knowledge of the community by citing some of its purposes. The most frequently mentioned purposes were mutual economic assistance and development of intracommunity trade. Only 4 percent of those who had read or heard of the community thought it was a forerunner of a United States of Europe.

Four out of ten people interviewed could name one or more of the EC member countries. The countries named most often were France, Great Britain, and Germany.

Only 5 percent of those who said they were acquainted with the community knew that the community's population was greater than that of the United States, that the community produces fewer goods than the United States, that the community exports more than the United States, and that the community's industrial production is growing faster than that of the United States.

Trust and Ties

Before inquiring directly about views toward the community, Gallup asked the respondents their attitudes toward various nationalities, their identification with different geographical areas, and their opinions on the US role in the world and on United States–European relations.

The survey showed that American attitudes toward the nationalities of the European Community seem to be more favorable than toward the people of all other countries except Switzerland.

The Gallup survey suggests that most Americans identify most strongly with their local neighborhood or with the United States. Only about one person in ten identified strongly with either "the Western world" or "the world as a whole." . . .

A majority (55 percent) of those interviewed felt that the United States should "stop getting involved in other countries' affairs." Thirty-eight percent said the United States must "play a leading role in world affairs." Seven percent had no opinion.

On the other hand, 65 percent of the people interviewed believed that US ties with Western Europe "matter a great deal." Only 16 percent said these ties are not important. The more the respondent knew about the Common Market, the survey found, the more important the respondent considered US ties with Western Europe.

The reasons most frequently given for the view that US ties with Western Europe "matter a great deal" were (in order of frequency):

The United States should remain interested in world affairs. "We should not isolate ourselves."

US-EC ties provide a stronger defense against communism.

It is important for trade. "We need to export and import."

"We need economic ties. Our growth is affected by Western Europe."

"We have the same cultures, the same ancestors."

Reasons given for saying that US ties with Western Europe "aren't very important" included:

"We should straighten out our own problems first."

"It is more to their advantage than ours."

Opinion on whether the United States should go to war, if necessary, to help defend Western Europe was about evenly divided. Forty-three percent said "no," 41 percent said "yes." Those who were unacquainted with the community were more inclined to reply in the negative, the survey found.

FROM "GRAND DESIGN" TO TROUBLED PARTNERSHIP [2]

Throughout the gestation of the Common Market and Euratom [European Atomic Energy Community], Washington remained in the background. President Dwight D. Eisenhower and other American leaders welcomed the growth of the new European institutions, but the United States played no direct role in the negotiations. The most important US gesture was its February 1957 pledge to supply Euratom with nuclear fuel and technical assistance.

The aloofness of the United States stemmed not only from chagrin over the rebuff of the EDC [European Defense Community] but also from its preoccupations with events outside Europe. On October 4, 1957, the Soviet Union orbited the world's first artificial satellite, Sputnik I, opening the space age. This demonstration of Soviet technolog-

[2] From *A Short Chronicle of United States–European Community Relations*, by Boyd France, international affairs correspondent in Washington for McGraw-Hill Publications. European Community Information Service. 2100 M Street, N.W. Washington, D.C. 20037. Ja. '73. p 23-30.

ical mastery shocked American leaders into another agoniz-
ing reappraisal. It bred fears of a "missile gap" and touched
off a frantic US effort to catch up and surpass the Soviets
in rocketry and space technology.

Cold War Resurgence

A new and searing Berlin crisis focused American attention on Europe briefly in 1959. It was defused by Eisenhower and Nikita S. Khrushchev, Soviet Communist party
chairman, at Camp David in September of that year, but
the "spirit of Camp David" vanished quickly. In June 1960,
Khrushchev snubbed Eisenhower at the abortive summit
conference in Paris after Eisenhower admitted US owner-
ship of the U-2 reconnaissance plane downed over Soviet
territory in May. In September the Soviet leader, banging
his shoe on his desk at the General Assembly of the United
Nations in New York, denounced the United States and all
its works. On the same trip, he embraced Cuba's Fidel
Castro. At the same time, the United States, mired in the
chaos of the Congo as the main organizer of the United
Nations peace-keeping force, found itself opposed by some
of its European allies.

By the time John Fitzgerald Kennedy assumed the
presidency in 1961, the American struggle to contain communism had spread to large areas of Asia, Africa, and Latin
America. Kennedy massively reinforced US aid programs
to counter Soviet aid recently supplemented by aid from
the more militantly revolutionary Chinese people's republic.

Only a few months in office, Kennedy was humiliated in
the Bay of Pigs invasion of Cuba. This crisis surmounted,
he confronted Khrushchev at Vienna, balked Soviet tanks at
point-blank range in Berlin, and launched the Alliance for
Progress. Then came the grim week in October 1962 when
the world trembled on the brink of nuclear war as Kennedy
insisted on the withdrawal of Soviet nuclear missiles from
Cuba.

The "Grand Design" Emerges

Embattled on a global scale against a seemingly monolithic Communist drive to take over the world, Kennedy and his advisers began to see Europe—stable, prosperous, and advancing toward unity—in a different light. No longer a helpless invalid dependent upon America for its survival, Europe began to look like a potentially strong partner in the global struggle against communism but also like a potential threat to US economic interests.

As early as December 1961, Secretary of State Dean Rusk spoke of a "grand design" of constructive association between the United States and a uniting Europe. To give this dream substance, Kennedy asked the Congress for the most sweeping authority ever requested by an American President to negotiate reductions in trade barriers. This Trade Expansion Act of 1962 envisaged free trade in most industrial goods between the United States and a Common Market expanded to include the United Kingdom.

The Trade Expansion Act was designed to provide an economic foundation for a political partnership between the United States and a uniting Europe. It was also aimed at lowering the level of discrimination against US exports to Europe represented by the common external tariff being put into place around the Common Market's six member countries. Kennedy, sending his trade legislation to the Congress, sounded both themes. Calling for a broad Atlantic partnership he said that "a freer flow of trade across the Atlantic will enable the two giant markets on either side of the ocean to impart strength and vigor to each other and to combine their resources and momentum to undertake the many enterprises which the security of free peoples demands."

Common Market a Threat

Kennedy also expressed concern over the impact of the emerging Common Market on the US economy if the common external tariff were not lowered in negotiation:

European manufacturers . . . have increased their share of this rapidly expanding market at a far greater rate than American manufacturers. Unless our industry can maintain, and increase, its share of this attractive market, there will be further temptation to locate additional American-financed plants in Europe in order to get behind the external tariff wall of the EEC. This would enable the American manufacturer to contend for that vast consumer potential on more competitive terms with his European counterparts, but it will also mean a failure on our part to take advantage of this growing market to increase jobs and investment in this country.

American concern over European discrimination against US products was aggravated by the steady deterioration of the US balance of payments. Yet trade worries did not dilute US support for European integration. The Kennedy Administration warmly welcomed Britain's belated decision to explore the possibilities of membership in the communities; negotiations began on November 8, 1961.

This welcoming attitude on the part of the United States contrasted with Washington's earlier lack of enthusiasm for Britain's role of leadership in the formation of the seven-nation European Free Trade Association. [The seven were Britain, Norway, Sweden, Portugal, Switzerland, Austria, Iceland; Finland later became an associate.—Ed.] Washington had also opposed British efforts to "build bridges" between the six and the seven by negotiating limited reciprocal tariff concessions between them. Unlike these purely commercial arrangements, British membership in the communities would bring political advantages that would compensate for any additional discrimination against US trade, in the view of the United States in the early sixties.

Economic Frictions Arise

Nevertheless, economic frictions flared in 1962 when the Trade Expansion Act was still new and the Kennedy Round of negotiations within the General Agreement on Tariffs and Trade (GATT) had not yet begun. The "chicken war" broke out between Washington and Brussels, the site of EEC headquarters. The dispute started when Brussels imposed supplemental charges on imported frozen chicken for which the United States had developed a large market in Europe. US chicken exports plummeted. Washington protested in vain. In 1963 the United States, acting within its GATT rights, retaliated by raising duties on several European products. The chicken war was over, but it was only the first of a series of skirmishes over the community's Common Agricultural Policy [CAP] which Washington still insists is unjustifiably protectionist and restrictive of US farm exports to the Common Market.

The chicken war looked minor next to the grave political confrontation between Washington and Paris after President Charles de Gaulle's abrupt January 14, 1963, veto of Britain's bid for Common Market membership. This confrontation severely tested the political cohesion of a European Community whose sympathies were divided between Washington and Paris. It also led the Kennedy Administration to reevaluate the "grand design" for Atlantic partnership.

Kennedy responded to de Gaulle's move by pressing the Europeans for ever tighter integration of their forces within the North Atlantic Treaty Organization (NATO). Kennedy also revived an earlier plan for an integrated NATO surface fleet armed with Polaris nuclear missiles. The official rationale for this multilateral force (MLF) was that it was the only politically acceptable way of associating Germany with allied decision making, a goal which Washington suggested was being insisted upon by Germany.

MLF Fails

The plan was widely condemned in Britain and the smaller allied states. The German government supported it, probably as much out of deference to Washington as out of conviction. De Gaulle recognized that Washington's nuclear fleet would downgrade his own embryonic nuclear *force de frappe*.

From June 1964 on, President Lyndon B. Johnson

pushed the MLF full speed ahead, but in December of that year he abruptly concluded that the MLF would never float. After a secret consultation with German Chancellor Ludwig Erhard, Johnson dispatched a confidential cable to his European ambassadors ordering them to cease lobbying for the MLF. The project sank without a ripple, marking the failure of the second American attempt to intervene in the sensitive politics of European defense.

The Kennedy Round negotiations had opened in Geneva on May 4, 1964, and were lurching from crisis to crisis. Announced with much fanfare as the bravest advance yet towards Atlantic partnership, the talks quickly turned into an Indian wrestling match between the United States and the Common Market over endless issues of commercial advantage.

The Common Market showed strength in surviving intact the pressures of negotiations at a time of internal dissension between France and the other five members over agricultural policy and the powers of the Common Market Commission. The community's weakness also showed in the difficulties and delays in getting agreement among the six member governments on a common negotiating mandate for the Commission, designated by the Common Market treaty as the sole negotiating agent for the community in trade matters.

Further Setbacks

The Kennedy Round was brought to a successful conclusion on June 30, 1967, hours before the US negotiating authority under the Trade Expansion Act expired. The outcome was hailed as the greatest blow against protectionism in history and a triumph for Atlantic partnership. It would be the last advance on the trade front for many years.

Successive Congresses refused to ratify the auxiliary Kennedy Round agreement for the elimination of the American Selling Price (ASP), a system of assessing duties on certain benzenoid chemicals. Repeal of ASP was important to the

Europeans in itself and also as a symbolic measure of American willingess to eliminate nontariff trade barriers. After three times extending the agreement, the community, in December 1972, allowed it to expire. The issue will come up again in the next round of GATT negotiations.

Both Johnson and President Richard M. Nixon repeatedly failed to win from Congress new negotiating authority to lower trade barriers. During the last two years of Nixon's first term of office (1968-72), protectionist pressure mounted feverishly in Congress, fueled by high unemployment and ballooning trade deficits.

The rising stridence of protectionist voices in Congress, the American labor movement, and some business sectors now increasingly found an echo within the Administration, raising questions about the US ability to lead another assault on trade obstacles, once again threatening to divide the United States politically from its allies.

US–EC Relations Mark Time

United States–European political relations marked time during the period between Johnson's decision to abandon the MLF and Nixon's dramatic moves during his trip to Paris in February 1969 to try to restore warm relations with the French government.

Johnson repeatedly affirmed US support for European unification, but during his term of office unification itself progressed haltingly, hobbled by internal political dissension. The paralysis was symbolized by General de Gaulle's second veto of British membership, on December 19, 1967. Again, France incurred the wrath of its five partners and indirectly that of the United States.

Preoccupied by the Vietnam war, Johnson increasingly resented the lack of European support for what he regarded as the US peace-keeping effort in Southeast Asia. The difference in the US and European official perspectives on the war underlined the built-in limits on the reach of the Atlantic partnership. So, too, had the six-day war of June 1967 in the Middle East, which brought discordant reactions from Washington and European capitals.

Nixon, in his first four years in office, found few opportunities for new departures in United States–European collaboration.

In Europe, West German Chancellor Willy Brandt had embarked upon his campaign to restore relations with East Germany and East European governments. Both EEC and EFTA [European Free Trade Association] governments' diplomatic energies were focused, from the summer of 1970 on, upon the renewed negotiations for membership of Britain, Denmark, Norway, and Ireland in the European communities.

Official Support of Europe Stressed

This time the United States played a role of benevolent bystander. Nixon was busy not only with the Vietnam war but also with restoring contact with the People's Republic of China, after a twenty-year hiatus, and with laying the political foundation for cooperation with the Soviet Union.

Nixon, however, like his predecessors, repeatedly stressed the primary importance of the United States–European partnership. He steadfastly rebuffed congressional pressure for unilateral withdrawal of US troops from Europe. In addition, he forged close personal relations with French President Georges Pompidou, British Prime Minister Edward Heath, Chancellor Brandt, and other European leaders. These personal contacts proved invaluable in deflecting a clash between the United States and Europe after the monetary crisis of August 1971, when Nixon decided to suspend convertibility of the dollar into gold and to impose a 10 percent temporary surcharge on imports.

Nixon reaffirmed US support for the European Community and its enlargement from the outset of his presidency. In his first foreign policy report to the Congress in February 1970, the President said:

As we move from dominance to partnership, there is the possibility that some will see this as a step toward disengagement. But in the third decade of our commitment to Europe, the depth of our relationship is a fact of life. We can no more disengage from Europe than from Alaska. . . .

We favor a definition by Europe of a distinct identity, for the sake of its own continued vitality and independence of spirit. Our support for the strengthening and broadening of the European Community has not diminished. We recognize that our interest will necessarily be affected by Europe's evolution, and we may have to make sacrifices in the common interest. We consider that the possible economic price of a truly unified Europe is outweighed by the gain in the political vitality of the West as a whole.

Raising Level of Diplomatic Relations

However, as the US dollar drain continued and the nation incurred its first trade deficit in a century the economic price for a unified Europe of ten instead of six began to look higher.

To keep minor differences in perspective, the United States and the European Community have steadily multiplied their channels of communication and diplomatic relations. In 1971, the communities' office in Washington was elevated to the diplomatic status of a "delegation." Over the years, exchanges of missions between the US Congress and the European Parliament have broadened mutual understanding at the political level. Each president of the ECSC [European Coal and Steel Community] High Authority and the EC and Euratom Commissions paid a state visit to Washington. President Nixon conferred with the EC Commission in Brussels in 1969. Regular confidential reviews of economic problems dividing the community and the United States were begun early in the Nixon Administration and have continued since.

Despite these efforts to improve mutual understanding, economic tensions between Washington and Brussels have not eased. To counter this trend, [Jean] Monnet's action committee has proposed institutionalizing the dialogue between the United States and the community, but so far this suggestion has not been acted upon.

As Nixon's second term began, the leeway for marking time in United States–European Community relations had clearly run out. Washington and Brussels stood at a cross-roads in the journey back from the ruins of World War II.

The enlargement of the community opened a new chapter in its evolution, rich with both political opportunities and risks for both Europe and the United States. Economically it poses new competitive challenges for the United States which could either push protectionist pressures past the explosion point or, conversely, trigger a new counter-attack on protectionism as happened in similar circumstances with the passage of the Trade Expansion Act in 1962. At stake will be the US ability to continue to support Europe militarily.

A "Declaration of Interdependence"

President Nixon recognized both challenges and risks of the community's enlargement in his message to the EC Commission which took office on January 6, 1973:

On behalf of the United States, I am pleased to assure you, as you begin your new duties, of our continued interest in a constructive relationship with the community. We face major common tasks and an unparalleled opportunity to build a more equitable and open international economic order. I am confident that, through close cooperation, our efforts will achieve success.

The tension in US–EC relations comes as the balance of power and interest between East and West is shifting in Europe. In this state of flux, the question arises of whether Washington and Brussels will continue to subordinate their individual interests to the common interest in the absence of an external threat. In the balance will be President Kennedy's vision of Atlantic partnership, outlined in his Independence Day speech in Philadelphia in 1962:

We do not regard a strong and united Europe as a rival but a partner . . . capable of playing a greater role in the common defense, of responding more generously to the needs of poorer nations, of joining with the United States and others in lowering trade barriers, resolving problems of commerce and commodities and currency, and developing coordinated policies in all economic and diplomatic areas . . . .

The United States will be ready for a declaration of interdependence. . . . We will be prepared to discuss with a united Europe the ways and means of forming an Atlantic partnership . . . between the new union emerging in Europe and the old American union founded here 175 years ago.

A NEW ATLANTIC CHARTER [3]

This year has been called the Year of Europe, but not because Europe was less important in 1972 or in 1969. The alliance between the United States and Europe has been the cornerstone of all postwar foreign policy. It provided the political framework for American engagements in Europe and marked the definitive end of US isolationism. It insured the sense of security that allowed Europe to recover from the devastation of the war. It reconciled former enemies. It was the stimulus for an unprecedented endeavor in European unity and the principal means to forge the common policies that safeguarded Western security in an era of prolonged tension and confrontation. Our values, our goals, and our basic interests are most closely identified with those of Europe.

A New Era

Nineteen seventy-three is the Year of Europe because the era that was shaped by decisions of a generation ago is ending. The success of those policies has produced new realities that require new approaches:

[3] From "1973: The Year of Europe," address at the annual meeting of the Associated Press editors, New York City, April 23, 1973, by Secretary of State Henry A. Kissinger (then assistant to the President for foreign affairs). Text from Department of State Publication 8710. Supt. of Docs. Washington, D.C. 20402. Je. '73.

The revival of Western Europe is an established fact, as is the historic success of its movement toward economic unification.

The East-West strategic military balance has shifted from American preponderance to near equality, bringing with it the necessity for a new understanding of the requirements of our common security.

Other areas of the world have grown in importance. Japan has emerged as a major power center. In many fields, "Atlantic" solutions to be viable must include Japan.

We are in a period of relaxation of tensions. But as the rigid divisions of the past two decades diminish, new assertions of national identity and national rivalry emerge.

Problems have arisen, unforeseen a generation ago, which require new types of cooperative action. Insuring the supply of energy for industrialized nations is an example.

These factors have produced a dramatic transformation of the psychological climate in the West—a change which is the most profound current challenge to Western statesmanship. In Europe, a new generation—to whom war and its dislocations are not personal experiences—takes stability for granted. But it is less committed to the unity that made peace possible and to the effort required to maintain it. In the United States, decades of global burdens have fostered, and the frustrations of the war in Southeast Asia have accentuated, a reluctance to sustain global involvements on the basis of preponderant American responsibility.

Inevitably this period of transition will have its strains. There have been complaints in America that Europe ignores its wider responsibilities in pursuing economic self-interest too one-sidedly and that Europe is not carrying its fair share of the burden of the common defense. There have been complaints in Europe that America is out to divide Europe economically, or to desert Europe militarily, or to bypass Europe diplomatically. Europeans appeal to the United States to accept their independence and their occasionally severe criticism of us in the name of Atlantic unity, while at the same time they ask for a veto on our independent policies—also in the name of Atlantic unity.

Our challenge is whether a unity forged by a common perception of danger can draw new purpose from shared positive aspirations.

If we permit the Atlantic partnership to atrophy, or to erode through neglect, carelessness, or mistrust, we risk what has been achieved, and we shall miss our historic opportunity for even greater achievement.

In the forties and fifties the task was economic reconstruction and security against the danger of attack. The West responded with courage and imagination. Today the need is to make the Atlantic relationship as dynamic a force in building a new structure of peace, less geared to crisis and more conscious of opportunities, drawing its inspirations from its goals rather than its fears. The Atlantic nations must join in a fresh act of creation, equal to that undertaken by the postwar generation of leaders of Europe and America. . . .

The United States proposes to its Atlantic partners that, by the time the President travels to Europe toward the end of the year [1973], we will have worked out a new Atlantic Charter setting the goals for the future. . . . [The President's trip was subsequently canceled.—Ed.]

Problems in Atlantic Relationships

The problems in Atlantic relationships are real. They have arisen in part because during the fifties and sixties the Atlantic Community organized itself in different ways in the many different dimensions of its common enterprise.

In economic relations, the European Community has increasingly stressed its regional personality; the United

States, at the same time, must act as part of, and be responsible for, a wider international trade and monetary system. We must reconcile these two perspectives.

In our collective defense, we are still organized on the principle of unity and integration, but in radically different strategic conditions. The full implications of this change have yet to be faced.

Diplomacy is the subject of frequent consultations but is essentially being conducted by traditional nation-states. The United States has global interests and responsibilities. Our European allies have regional interests. These are not necessarily in conflict, but in the new era neither are they automatically identical. . . .

Agenda for the Future

No element of American postwar policy has been more consistent than our support of European unity. We encouraged it at every turn. We knew that a united Europe would be a more independent partner. But we assumed, perhaps too uncritically, that our common interests would be assured by our long history of cooperation. We expected that political unity would follow economic integration; and that a unified Europe working cooperatively with us in an Atlantic partnership would ease many of our international burdens.

It is clear that many of these expectations are not being fulfilled.

The United States and Europe have benefited from European economic integration. Increased trade within Europe has stimulated the growth of European economies and the expansion of trade in both directions across the Atlantic.

But we cannot ignore the fact that Europe's economic success and its transformation from a recipient of our aid to a strong competitor has produced a certain amount of friction. There have been turbulence and a sense of rivalry in international monetary relations. . . .

The gradual accumulation of sometimes petty, sometimes major, economic disputes must be ended and be replaced by a determined commitment on both sides of the Atlantic to find cooperative solutions.

The United States will continue to support the unification of Europe. We have no intention of destroying what we worked so hard to help build. For us, European unity is what it has always been: not an end in itself but a means to the strengthening of the West. We shall continue to support European unity as a component of a larger Atlantic partnership.

PARTNERSHIP OR "PAX AMERICANA"? [4]

A speech's life expectancy normally coincides with de Gaulle's dictum on treaties: Like young girls and roses, they last as long as they last. While Dr. Kissinger's April 23 [1973] talk to the Associated Press editors is covered by almost six months of dust, it provoked questions and reactions that persist. These issues include: the linkage among the questions to be dealt with, the accusation of Europe as a regional bloc, the differences in perspective between Europe and the United States, the role of Japan, the ability of the European countries to work out a common approach, and, most importantly, whether the United States really wants such a common approach.

The principal European reaction to the speech has been confusion: puzzlement over the obscurity of the Administration's first attempt to amplify its new slogan, "1973—the Year of Europe." Nonetheless, Europeans are agreed that it is better to have had the speech than no speech at all; in theory, any attention by Washington is a good thing. Whether this is sound can be debated.

Given its 1941 namesake, the reference to "Atlantic Charter" proved at once to be an unhappy formulation. The

[4] From article, "Some European Questions for Dr. Kissinger," by J. Robert Schaetzel, former United States Ambassador to the European Community (1966-1972). *Foreign Policy.* 12:66-8, 70-4. Fall '73. Reprinted with permission from *Foreign Policy* 12 © 1973 by National Affairs, Inc.

Germans could hardly be pleased, the French were instantly irritated. During Chancellor Brandt's May visit to Washington, President Nixon disassociated himself from the notion, suggesting that Kissinger had thrown it in on his own authority. Curiously and simultaneously his spokesmen in Europe defended Kissinger with the argument that it was Nixon who had insisted on insertion of the "new Atlantic Charter" concept. The end result was more confusion. . . .

Europeans resent Kissinger's self-serving allusion to Europe's regional preoccupations and role, as contrasted to the global responsibilities of the United States. By unhappy timing, the 1973 Foreign Policy Report of the President, known to have been written under Kissinger's supervision, came out ten days after the New York speech. Piecing the speech and the report together, Europeans detected nothing less than an Administration attack on the European Community. They saw at once that the traditional American litany of support for European unity was cast in the past tense while the references to the present and future stressed the "European Community's increasingly regional economic policies."

Ignorance or Indifference?

The speech demonstrated either America's lack of seriousness about, or gross ignorance of, Western Europe's situation and problems, in that it laid down a totally unrealistic time schedule: The proposed trip by the President in the fall of 1973 [subsequently canceled] allowed no more than six months for European preparation of a common position on the political, defense, and economic issues, and the development of a new Atlantic Charter. In October 1972, the original and the prospective members of the European Community held their summit meeting in Paris on the future of the community. Despite a more limited purpose and agenda, European foreign ministers and high officials had devoted more than a year of preparation for this meeting. The Europeans find it difficult to believe that Washington ould be unaware of this, or of the major organizational problems of the new community of nine. . . .

In general, European reaction to the speech has been confused, skeptical and critical—in that order. In their search for explanation and motive some cynical Europeans dismiss the speech as one part of a White House strategy to divert attention from the spreading scandal of Watergate.

Some Positive Thinking

A few, including some of the critics, continue to search for and attempt to exploit the favorable aspects. The Europeans' effort to develop a positive response to the United States has two strong motivations: first, to ease the tense and potentially dangerous Atlantic situation; second, to exploit the speech as an external force to move the Europeans to act in unison. . . .

Corrections and Clarifications

Europeans have been struck by the stream of "clarifications" about the speech coming from the White House and Kissinger—even from the always timid and generally uninformed State Department. As the Europeans have questioned or criticized a part of the speech—linkage, Europe as a regional economic bloc, the new pentagonal balance of power system, the new Atlantic Charter and the implied threat of withdrawal of forces—at each point the White House has denied that this was what was meant. Another stone in this arch of confusion was Secretary [of the Treasury George P.] Shultz's opening testimony before the Ways and Means Committee in which he insisted that in the anticipated trade negotiations, the United States would not be content with reciprocity; it expects to get more than it gave. Immediately the Administration scrambled to "correct" this statement with a subordinate official, William Eberle, the trade negotiator, asserting that of course the United States remained committed to full balance and reciprocity. For years the Administration has centered its fire against the barriers to American agricultural goods set up by the European Community. At the crucial point—literally hours before the Council of Ministers determined the community's basic position for the trade negotiations—Washington, without any advance notice or sensitivity to the foreign impact, slapped an embargo on soy products and cottonseed meal. . . .

While the general reaction has been to dismiss the speech as hastily written and poorly conceived, many Europeans, in whose education Machiavelli played a significant role, detect a more sinister ploy. Some of these with long acquaintance with Kissinger and his thoughts, find it hard to accept the simplistic explanation of a busy official distracted by other pressing business and thus forced to throw away an off-the-cuff address before the Associated Press. They divine, first of all, a clever ruse. The sheer ambiguity of the speech allows Washington a 360-degree range of options—from engaging Europe in a thorough-going renovation of the Atlantic relationship, on America's terms, to justifying American retrenchment and closer relations with Russia in the face of "proven" Western European intransigence. Second, a few see this as an underhanded attack on European unity: the scope of the agenda, an impossible time schedule with a demand for a European reaction, can only intensify internal European disagreement. With the increase in pressure the centrifugal forces in Europe would be strengthened, driving the individual nations to deal with Washington bilaterally, as Kissinger had always wished. The end result would be to bury an Atlantic partnership of equals and to revive the Atlantic Community, meaning "Pax Americana."

TRADE—A MAJOR BONE OF CONTENTION [5]

The United States makes no secret of its unhappiness with a number of the European Community's policies on the grounds that they violate the principles of reciprocity and freer trade. In future trade negotiations the United States hopes to persuade the community to modify the practices we find most objectionable and to agree to revise the present trading rules known as the General Agreement on Tariffs and Trade (GATT). GATT, which is subscribed to by some eighty nations and governs 85 percent of world trade, has been in effect since 1948.

US concern over the state of our trade relations with the European Community as well as with our other major trading partners, Canada and Japan, has been growing for some time. Our anxiety peaked in 1971 when our world trade account sank into the red for the first time since 1888 with a deficit of $2.9 billion. (The six, however, as in years past, imported more from the United States than they sold.)

Although the United States laid much of the blame for its trade crisis on its partners, there were other major contributing factors. The growth rate of the US economy has lagged behind that of our major competitors. Our productivity has grown at a slower pace—although our workers still turn out at least 20 percent more goods and services per man-hour than workers in other leading nations. With the rapid dissemination of science and technology, US industry has lost some of the technological and managerial lead it formerly enjoyed. The post-1965 inflation and the overvaluation of the dollar in relation to other currencies (prior to the December 1971 realignment) increased the demand for imports and damaged the competitiveness of US exports.

Temporary factors peculiar to 1971 also played a role in transforming our traditional trade surplus into a deficit. . . .

[5] From *Great Decisions 1973*. Topic No. 5: "The Common Market Expands: Can the U.S. Compete?" Foreign Policy Association. 345 E. 46th St. New York 10017. '73. p 54-6. Reprinted with permission from *Great Decisions 1973*. Copyright 1973 by the Foreign Policy Association, Inc.

For all these reasons, US trade in 1971 was in deep trouble. Without a trade surplus to help offset the outflow of dollars for military expenditures, corporate investment overseas, tourism and other nontrade items, the deficit in our international payments plummeted to an annual rate of $9.3 billion.

New Economic Policy

The economic crisis prompted the President to take emergency measures in mid-August 1971. The new economic policy was designed, among other things, to shore up the dollar and combat speculation, to pave the way for a realignment of foreign exchange rates, to boost exports and slow down imports. The new policy imposed a 10 percent surcharge on all dutiable imports; it called on Congress to provide a "buy American" 10 percent tax credit to US manufacturers investing in US-made industrial equipment; it severed the link between the dollar and gold by halting the convertibility of dollar holdings of foreign governments.

Some of the emergency measures were rescinded in December 1971 after hard bargaining between the United States and the other major economic powers. The first inkling that a breakthrough was near came during President Nixon's summit meeting with President Pompidou in the Azores. President Nixon declared that the United States was prepared to devalue the dollar in terms of gold (he had previously opposed such a step) as part of a general realignment of exchange rates. Pompidou, in turn, withdrew his earlier objections to trade talks with the United States and agreed to include on the agenda concessions the United States wanted from the European Community.

Monetary Reform

After further discussions in Washington among the finance ministers of the leading industrial nations, known as the Group of Ten, the President on December 18 announced what he termed "the most significant monetary agreement in the history of the world." The United States raised the official price of gold from $35 to $38 an ounce, the first change in the official value of gold since 1934, and a number of other countries revalued their currencies upward. The net result: an effective devaluation of the dollar by 12 percent. The Administration claimed this would enable the United States to increase its exports by at least $6 billion to $9 billion a year and raise domestic employment by some 500,000 to 750,000 jobs.

The monetary agreement which the President unveiled with such fanfare at the Smithsonian Institution was, in fact, a stopgap measure. It signaled the demise of the old international monetary system designed at Bretton Woods, New Hampshire in 1944, but it created no substitute. It primarily underscored the need for a new system and for new rules of international exchange. . . .

Trade Priorities

One of the principal items on the US trade agenda . . . , which could determine the course of world commerce for years to come, is our grievances against the European Community. Our complaints run the gamut from Europe's alleged indifference to our economic difficulties to the barriers we claim the Common Market has erected around its ever-expanding trade bloc at the expense of the United States and other nonmembers.

A prime object of our discontent is the community's Common Agricultural Policy, which affects over 95 percent (by value) of the six's produce and will eventually affect a comparable amount in all nine countries. Since the Common Agricultural Policy was adopted, US exports to the community of those commodities covered by the policy, notably grains, citrus fruit, tobacco, poultry and lard, have declined. Other agricultural exports, however, have increased, and the Common Market remains the US farmer's best foreign customer.

New Headaches

The entry of Britain, the world's largest food importer, into the community promises to compound US producers' woes. Lured by higher prices, British farmers will begin producing more; other agricultural needs, notably feed grains, will be filled by duty-free imports from the community. This outlook is not designed to raise the spirits of Britain's traditional suppliers, the United States among them.

If agriculture were not so important to the United States, Washington could shrug off the prospective loss of customers. But agricultural products constitute almost one fifth of our total exports. The crop from one out of five acres harvested in the United States is sold abroad and provides about one seventh of total US farm income. Furthermore, US agriculture is a highly efficient growth industry. Had it not been for a substantial surge in US agricultural exports in 1971, with record sales to the community, the trade picture would have been even bleaker. Agricultural goods accounted for almost 60 percent of the total increase in exports that year.

Thanks to the efficiency and high productivity of our farmers, our products continue to be competitive in world markets. They are competitive, that is, when they are not up against barriers such as the community's variable levy. In the forthcoming trade negotiations, a major US goal is to get better terms for our agricultural exports, in part by persuading the community to reduce its protection and halt its dumping of surpluses in our traditional markets.

Nontariff Barriers

After agriculture, the second major item on the US agenda is the reduction of the community's nontariff barriers to trade. Nontariff barriers fall into three categories: those that impede imports; those that provide assistance to domestic producers; and those that provide direct economic aid to exporters. According to a GATT survey, its members impose some eight hundred such obstacles to free trade.

Among the community's trade barriers which we find most objectionable (though we ourselves impose many of the same restrictions) are quotas, export promotion devices, export subsidies, customs procedures and valuation methods, product and safety standards and testing requirements which disqualify US exports. The community, for example, is in the process of developing a uniform standard for electronic and electrical products. Washington is convinced that one object of the exercise is to exclude a wide variety of US goods.

Preferential Agreements

Our third major grievance is the preferential trading arrangements and association agreements the community has concluded with more than thirty countries. The United States complains that these agreements discriminate against nonmembers, distort trading patterns (they hurt US citrus fruit and tobacco sales) and violate the most-favored-nation principle, namely that a trade concession made to one country must be extended to all.

The community's network of special trading arrangements encompasses primarily less-developed countries in Africa and the Mediterranean region. The agreements provide duty-free access to the community for certain goods; in return, selected community exports receive preferred treatment, known as reverse preferences.

The network is being expanded. The community in July [1972] negotiated treaties with six EFTA countries which did not follow their associates—Britain and Denmark —into the Common Market. The trade treaties with these six countries—Austria, Finland, Iceland, Portugal, Sweden and Switzerland—provide for duty-free trade in industrial goods within five years.

The community's objective in building this giant preferential trading zone, stretching from the North Cape through

Europe to Southern Africa, many Americans are convinced, is not to encourage world trade but to monopolize as much of it as possible for its own advantage. In the forthcoming negotiations, the United States will ask the nine to prove that this is not the case, that they are still committed to trade liberalization. They can do this either by observing the most-favored-nation principle and granting the United States the same concessions they grant others or by offering the United States compensation for the trade we lose as a result of the preferential accords.

REFLECTIONS ON THE YEAR THAT WAS (NOT) [6]

Last January President Richard M. Nixon tossed off the phrase "the Year of Europe." The thought behind the President's rhetoric was simple: "peace with honor" had terminated US military involvement in Vietnam; the foundations of a triangular superpower policy had been laid with the Peking and Moscow visits; therefore Washington could turn its attention to Western Europe and Japan. Such issues as trade, defense, and mutual and balanced force reductions between the North Atlantic Treaty Organization (NATO) and the Warsaw Pact would in 1973 be "on the front burner," in President Nixon's words at his January 31 [1973] news conference. In then presidential assistant Henry A. Kissinger's *cordon bleu* cuisine, where only one dish can be cooked on one burner at a time, it was fitting that Europe should have its special year.

For Europe, of course, every year is a Year of Europe. If 1973 was to have any special significance, it was not because the Americans were ready to end a long period of neglect. Rather, it was because 1973 was the year of the community's enlargement, the first year of the ambitious timetable for a full economic and monetary union, and the

[6] Reprint of " 'Year of Europe': Reflections on the Year That Was (Not)," article by Peter Jenkins, Washington correspondent for *The Guardian* (Manchester). *European Community.* 172:8-10. Ja. '74.

year in which the enlarged and fortified community would have the opportunity to speak with its European voice in the Conference on Security and Cooperation in Europe (CSCE).

As 1973 began, Europe and the United States thus had a basic conflict of perception and priority. The Europeans saw the chief problems on the transatlantic agenda as not new and already the subject of continuing discussion in the appropriate forum. A new round of trade negotiations in the General Agreement on Tariffs and Trade (GATT) was to be launched at a September ministerial meeting in Tokyo, and the community, more forward than the United States, had committed itself to agreement on a negotiating posture by midsummer. Reform of the international monetary system was underway, although trudgingly, in the International Monetary Fund (IMF), which had established a special committee for this purpose. NATO was at work on its busy agendas within its well-established institutions. In addition, a series of bilateral "summits" were being scheduled in the usual fashion following the election or reelection of a US President. All that seemed to be in question was the urgency and outcome of this work program.

The Americans focused on these problems as a cluster ﹁d saw them in a different light. Belated attention to the sues automatically created a sense of urgency. A whopping payments deficit, inflated by a trade deficit of unprecedented proportions, coupled with rising protectionist sentiment in the Congress, invested the Year of Europe with an air of crisis. Renewed attacks on the dollar, leading to a second devaluation and finally the replacement of the *ancien régime* by a floating regime, exacerbated these domestic pressures. In addition, reaction to US involvement in Southeast Asia could translate itself into a new isolationism opposed to any overseas commitments. The Year of Europe, it seemed in those early months, could well have become the year of Senator Mike Mansfield's resolution for US troop cutbacks in Europe.

Kissinger Calls for "New Atlantic Charter"

For the above reasons and with little regard for Europe's perceptions or preoccupations, the US Administration officials, most of them well disposed toward the Europe community and good US relations with it (the point should be stressed), urged that the pressing problems of trade, money, and defense burden sharing be attacked within some greater framework of political purpose. These officials (for example, the departing Secretary of Commerce, Peter G. Peterson) feared the result of leaving United States–European problems to the technical mercies of trade specialists. The most visible product of these urgings came in Kissinger's April 23 speech calling for a "new Atlantic Charter." The speech stressed that the problems within the Atlantic Community should be approached not only collectively but politically: they were too serious to be entrusted "solely to the experts," and their solution "must engage the top political leaders."

Kissinger's speech might have been better received if its spirit had been better understood. Conversely, it might have been better understood had he given concrete form to his general call to "revitalize" the Atlantic relationships and had he worked out the practical difficulties within the constructive context of a broadly redefined common purpose. It was tactfully explained at the time that the United States did not want to seem to be prejudging the issues by suggesting solutions, but the truth was that Washington had no solutions to propose.

It was symbolic that Kissinger's speech should have been delivered in the week in which the Watergate scandals broke in full force around the presidency. Thereafter, Watergate became an important factor in the diplomacy of the Year of Europe. No matter how often the denials in Washington and—with ever decreasing conviction—in the capitals of Europe, the Nixon Administration became inescapably immobilized. The President had committed himself to a "grand tour" of Europe to cap off the year and hankered persistently for a glorious "summit" conference of some kind to crown the event. He was suspected of seeking a diversion, of attaching more importance to form than to substance. In the United States the success or failure of the Year of Europe came to be seen in terms of whether or not the President would indeed go to Europe.

This false sense of urgency was created at a time when changes in the economic situation had removed some of the urgency. Following the dollar float, the American economy was surging happily back toward a trade surplus, and by the autumn the air of crisis which had marked the opening of the year had largely evaporated. With employment rising quickly, the pressures for protectionism lessened. In any case, the Congress was preoccupied with other matters.

Security Issues Pose Problem

Kissinger, however, remained irritated with the response to his call for a new Atlantic Charter, since watered down to a declaration of principle. In fact, there were to be at least two such declarations, one jointly by the United States and the European Community and the other by NATO. Kissinger's irritation stemmed largely from the Europeans' unwillingness and inability to deal with security matters in the same forum, or even on the same sheet of paper, as political and economic matters. Washington found the European attitude hard to understand, for the questions were indisputably linked. Too, there was the practical problem that differences with Europe over trade or money contributed to the Congress' reluctance to continue stationing the same number of troops in Europe without complete offset of the exchange costs. How could the Congress and the American public be persuaded otherwise if the Europeans seemed not to recognize the linkage of economics and security and appeared to seek shelter behind jurisdictional disputes?

The Americans were slow to see that the nine's draft declaration in Copenhagen in September did represent the first success of the enlarged community in achieving common positions on such an important subject of foreign policy as Atlantic relations, a subject which for ten years had bitterly divided them. But the Americans were quick to see that the document was of little worth in specifically answering the points raised by Kissinger in April. Its formulations were legalistic and lacked warmth. Even the word "partnership" had not been admitted. Kissinger eventually, however, gave a public welcome to the document and accepted it as the basis for further discussions. Parallel discussions were in progress in NATO.

These discussions appeared to go reasonably well until the Middle East crisis exploded. The Year of Europe was effectively wrecked. The American frustrations came pouring out. Chiefly they concerned the lack of political and military cooperation received from the NATO allies during the crisis. In the poisoned atmosphere, however, all manner of other nagging complaints were voiced—including US criticism over the preliminary GATT negotiations and alleged EC trade discriminations. When EC Commission Vice President Christopher Soames, responsible for the community's external relations, visited Washington in October, he had not been so bullied since a student at Eton.

The final casualty of the Year of Europe appears to have been the Nixon Administration's trade bill. A complicated muddle arose in which it became impossible to pass the measure without an amendment which would deny the President his existing power to give credits to the Soviet Union. The Administration's choice was to postpone the bill. Its prospects for early resuscitation seemed gloomy. European reaction was predictable.

Thus, what was to have been the Nixon Round in the GATT will, at best, be delayed. These important trade negotiations, linked both to the international monetary reform negotiations and, by the Americans, to the sharing of common defense costs, had been the centerpiece of the exercise known as the Year of Europe.

What Went Wrong?

The Year of Europe had ironically gone full circle. In the uneasy aftermath of the Atlantic crisis which broke around the Mideast war, the United States appeared to have no hesitation, still, when it came to choosing between détente with its adversary and the so-called equal partnership with its allies. It was Moscow first all the way. Ironically, it had been to correct this suspicion of superpower condominium, which he denied to be justified, that the President ten months earlier had proclaimed 1973 the Year of Europe.

What went wrong? Perhaps the basic mistake was to ask self-searching and somewhat abstract questions about a taken-for-granted relationship at a time when the relationship was under practical strains. It was not, in short, a good time to discuss the marriage. Events—notably the Mideast war, the energy crisis, and the constitutional crisis in Washington—rocked these shaky foundations for a new understanding. By the end of the year, Atlantic diplomacy had become an exercise in crisis management, an unfamiliar technique among allies.

Something will have been gained on both sides of the Atlantic, however, if the next Year of Europe can be conducted with clearer perceptions. The United States failed to understand (partly because of lack of communications between the State Department's professional bureaucracy and Kissinger's one-man band at the White House) that the community was experiencing the growing pains of its enlargement and was not capable of settling all its problems at the same time. The community was at a half-way stage—unhappy in its old client relationship with the United States but not yet able to be an independent partner. Europe could not answer the questions which Kissinger asked.

The Europeans, for their part, underestimated the Nixon Administration's problems with the Congress and public opinion, were insensitive to the American way of doing things (which is always by a sudden and massive assault on an outstanding problem), and failed to understand fully the American impatience for dividends from their long-term investment in European unity. Kissinger's questions were valid ones. The Europeans resented his distinction between Europe as a regional power and the United States as a global power. The Mideast crisis showed this distinction to be near the truth. That crisis, the climax of the Year of Europe, surely proved that a partnership of equals will remain impossible until a united Europe can deal collectively with the interlocked problems of economics, politics, and security.

A SHIFT IS IN THE CARDS [7]

Reprinted from *U.S. News & World Report.*

A change for the better in the long-troubled relations between the nine-member Common Market and the United States is being widely predicted.

One reason: The election of a new French president to succeed the late Georges Pompidou is expected to lead to a softening in the harsh anti-American line pursued by the Paris government for the past fifteen years.

Under Mr. Pompidou—and his illustrious predecessor, General Charles de Gaulle—France had worked determinedly to build the European Community into an economic and political rival to America.

Just hours before President Pompidou died on April 2 [1974], the French government demonstrated anew its determination to construct an anti-American Europe. The nine European foreign ministers, meeting in Luxembourg, were faced with these questions:

Is the Common Market to develop a full partnership with America, extending far beyond their joint defense commitment? Or is it to become an economic and political rival of the United States?

[7] From "U.S. Relations With Europe—A Shift Is in the Cards." *U.S. News & World Report.* 76:23-4. Ap. 15, '74.

Majority for United States

In the showdown, eight of the nine ministers came out solidly in favor of full partnership by supporting a plan to set up machinery for formal and regular consultation with the United States.

The eight clearly were heeding President Nixon's warning that the European allies cannot count indefinitely on American cooperation in mutual defense if they are bent on competing with the United States in other matters.

France alone voted "no." Foreign Minister Michel Jobert vetoed the plan for closer consultation with America on the ground that it would lead to Washington's domination of the Common Market and prevent Europe from developing its own independent "identity."

That has been the classic argument employed by French Gaullists in their long campaign to combat American influence in Europe—while, at the same time, looking to the United States for their security.

Now, with the death of President Pompidou, the picture is bound to change. France . . . still will be a difficult partner for the United States. But there is a reasonable chance that the extreme anti-American line other French governments have attempted to impose on the Common Market for the past fifteen years will be moderated.

The Paris bureau of *U.S. News & World Report* cabled this assessment:

"The presidential election could turn France in a new direction—toward closer consultation with its allies, both American and European."

Other developments in recent weeks also seem to insure that the Common Market will seek to avoid conflict with Washington.

In Britain, the new Labour government is committed to close collaboration with the United States—a striking contrast with the outgoing Conservative government under

Prime Minister Edward Heath. He had backed France's anti-American approach.

Britain's new foreign minister served notice on April 1 that cooperation with the United States is indispensable to an effective Atlantic alliance. He warned that if the British people believed that disagreement with America was inevitable, this "would adversely influence their attitude toward the development of the community."

German Support

A second development pointing to improved transatlantic cooperation is the strong stand by West Germany in favor of a firm institutional link between the European group and Washington. France stubbornly opposed the link.

Commenting on this German switch away from France and toward the United States, the Bonn correspondent of *U.S. News & World Report* cabled:

"For the first time in the quarter-century since Konrad Adenauer laid down the cardinal principle of close West German friendship with Paris, anti-French emotions here have risen to the point that they threaten to become official policy."

Thus, a new British–West German axis inside the Common Market is shifting the balance of power decisively against the kind of rivalry with Washington that French governments have advocated for fifteen years.

Already this axis, even when opposed by France, has defused many issues that have caused friction between the nine and the United States. Thus:

A French-sponsored scheme for special bilateral cooperation between the Common Market and the Arab oil-producing states remains blocked—at least until effective arrangements are made for consultations with Washington.

A Common Market plan to set up a preferential trading area in the Mediterranean region, Africa and the Far

East is being modified to meet American objections that US exports would be harmed.

A controversy over sharing of the mutual defense burden has been resolved. US Defense Secretary James R. Schlesinger says he is satisfied with a West German offer to cover most of the foreign exchange cost entailed in stationing more than 200,000 American servicemen in that country.

Nixon's Warning

What brought eight of nine Common Market members into closer harmony was President Nixon's warning on March 15:

"The Europeans cannot have it both ways. They cannot have the United States' participation and cooperation on the security front and then proceed to have confrontation and even hostility on the economic and political fronts."

All of the allies—even the French—recognize that the United States defense commitment is indispensable to their political, as well as their military, security.

Furthermore, they concede that there is no practical alternative. The nine Common Market countries together have population and economic wealth comparable to that of the United States, but a United States of Europe—one that could pool their manpower and industrial resources—is a rapidly fading dream.

A series of events in recent months has reversed the trend toward greater integration and plunged the European Community into disarray.

The goal of monetary and economic union by 1980 is virtually dead as a consequence of rampant inflation and the decisions of France, Britain and Italy to permit their currencies to "float" independently.

The Common Agriculture Policy—a cornerstone of the community—is under serious strain due to currency fluctuations and a demand by Britain for basic changes in the regulations.

Even the customs union formed by the nine countries was called into question by the refusal of the group to take a joint stand against an Arab oil embargo aimed at only one of its members—the Netherlands.

The controversy over cooperation or noncooperation with the United States added greatly to the disarray.

And now the new Labour government in London is threatening to call a popular referendum on the question of withdrawal from the Common Market if major changes are not made in Britain's favor.

The London correspondent of this magazine cabled:

"Three of five Britons express outright condemnation of this country's membership in the European Community. In consequence of this growing disenchantment, sentiment now is growing in Britain in favor of a looser form of grouping, largely based on a customs union, in which national sovereignty and economic independence are less circumscribed."

Uncertain Future

In other European capitals a question being seriously debated is not whether the Common Market can achieve unity but whether it can survive as anything more than a trading group.

A dispatch from the magazine's European economic correspondent reports: "Never since the Common Market came into being in 1958 have officials at its Brussels headquarters and in European capitals been more disillusioned and uncertain about the future of this organization."

He quotes official Swiss observers to the effect:

"The Common Market isn't going to pieces—not yet. But the Europe of the future, at best, will be a loosely tied coalition of sovereign states without a common political will."

For the United States, the message coming out of Europe at this time is clear:

Any further progress by the European Common Market toward political and economic union will have to be built on the basis of cooperation—not rivalry—with America if it is ever going to be built at all.

Eight of the nine member countries seem unwilling to advance on any other terms. Even the ninth—France—may soon no longer be the "odd man out."

TO BE AN EQUAL PARTNER, EUROPE MUST UNITE [8]

I earnestly believe that what we are seeking and groping for is a new level of equal partnership between the United States on the one hand and the European Community on the other. It will inevitably be a relationship of a totally different kind from what was the relationship between the United States and any one of the individual EC member countries before the creation of the community. To arrive at a situation of equal partnership is going to demand a high degree of understanding on both sides of the Atlantic.

First, let us consider it from the US point of view. The Americans, as I see it, must appreciate that the conception of a united Europe is not merely in order that the countries and the peoples of Europe should enrich themselves further. Rather, it is so that Europe, with all the long experience which goes so far back into the past, can bring that experience to bear on the major problems of the world, using that experience and offering it to the world in all the great problems which the world faces. This fact must be appreciated by the United States, which must understand that its relationship with Western Europe can no longer be the same as it was accustomed to between the United States and individual EC member countries.

Secondly, from the European point of view, I offer this

[8] From "Speaking Out on US-EC Relations: To Be an Equal Partner, Europe Must Unite," abridged version of address delivered to the European Parliament, January 16, 1974, by Sir Christopher Soames, a vice president of the Commission of the European Communities, responsible for external relations. *European Community*. 174:12. Mr. '74.

thought. When we talk about a dialogue between equal partners, Europe had better put itself in the position where it can be an equal partner. If Europe does not, it is Europe's own fault and no one else's. It is no good blaming other people. This does not mean merely that Europe can talk with one voice about commerce or about negotiations within the GATT. That is all very important, but is by no means enough. It means that we have to superimpose, and have the will to do so, in our national interests the realization that it is in all our interests that Europe should succeed. This means realizing that what may look bad in the tactical, immediate future for an individual country may be the right solution for Europe.

At the moment, Commission proposals on whatever topic—I do not say whether any particular proposals are good or bad—at least come out as European proposals and are conceived as such. They are then discussed in the Council of Ministers and in the member countries as national problems and are thrown into the national arena. What has to happen, if we are to ensure that the European interest dominates, is that somewhere along the line such proposals return to being discussed in a European context. Europe owes this not only to itself but to its partners.

But, at present, it is difficult for our partners. The European-American partnership-relationship covers an enormous spectrum. Yet on a large range of that spectrum we cannot talk with a European voice. It is difficult for the United States when it does not know to whom it should speak—and when it does speak to the chairman in office of the EC Council of Ministers, all he can say is, "I take note of what you say and I will report it to the Council of Ministers."

We have progressed. But how we progress, how we manage it, and what sort of concept we have are secondary compared with the basic realization that we must progress not only in our own interest but also if we are to get into a position in which we can claim to be equal partners.

V. LOOKING AHEAD TO 1980

EDITOR'S INTRODUCTION

Crystal-ball gazers disagree about the outlook for the Common Market. The *Wall Street Journal*'s London bureau correspondent, Robert Prinsky, ventures the prediction that if the Common Market merely survives these troubled times, it will have accomplished a great deal. The editor in chief of *Die Zeit* of Hamburg, Theo Sommer, is more optimistic. He is convinced that, after a difficult period, the European Community is on the move again. Bernard D. Nossiter of the Washington *Post* disagrees. He doubts that the Common Market will ever develop into anything more than it now is—strictly a convenient commercial arrangement.

The final selections present the views of three men who have been active in building Europe: West German Chancellor Helmut Schmidt, former EC Commissioner Ralf Dahrendorf, and Altiero Spinelli, commissioner in charge of industry and technology for the community. Their approaches differ but they foresee the same end—a stronger European Community.

NEW HOPE FOR UNITY? [1]

The black Citroën bearing France's new foreign minister swept up to the Charlemagne Building . . . [in Brussels] recently and reporters crowded around for a word or two from the new man, Jean Sauvagnargues, before he went in to preside over a Common Market [European Economic Community or EEC] foreign ministers' meeting.

After fielding a few questions in his native French, Mr.

[1] Reprint of "New Hope for the Common Market?" by Robert Prinsky, member of the London bureau. *Wall Street Journal.* p 8. Ag. 1, '74. Reprinted with permission of The Wall Street Journal © 1974 Dow Jones & Company, Inc. All Rights Reserved.

Sauvagnargues readily agreed to answer one in German for the benefit of a West German radio reporter's tape recorder. It was a tiny gesture, but a significant one when it is remembered that his Gaullist predecessor, the ultranationalist Michel Jobert, was perfectly capable of speaking a foreign language—English—but almost never did in public.

At a time when Common Market unity has been foundering on just about every important issue, France has developed a new, more cooperative stance toward its eight partners. This stance is one of the main symptoms—some say the only real cause—of a resurgence of optimism for the European Community's [EC's] future.

The optimists are extremely guarded, however, for last winter's gloom that enveloped the Eurocrats who work in Brussels can't be dissipated easily. Its causes still remain, as deeply embedded as ever: failure to form a common front toward Arab oil producers, failure to meet deadlines for closer economic integration, failure to launch a regional aid fund and Britain's doubts about remaining in the community.

But the optimism is being nurtured by some small signs of a willingness to cooperate. Such a will wasn't evident as recently as a few months ago.

For example, the Common Market agreed to a consultation procedure to keep Washington informed during its decision-making process. It also has improved its compensation offer to the United States and other nations for trade losses suffered due to Britain's joining. France long opposed both moves.

Italy has agreed to exempt agricultural produce other than beef from its import deposit requirement, thus patching up most of one breach in the frayed common farm policy. Also, some roadblocks to a community transport policy have been overcome.

Going Ahead but . . .

In other ways, normal community functions are going ahead. Officials press on with antitrust cases, their power undiminished by the political vacuum. New trade treaties continue to be implemented, like one recently with Uruguay. And the farm policy continues to find new ways to irk other nations; the United States and most other cattle-raising nations recently protested the EC's ban on beef imports in the face of a 140,000-ton European surplus.

Of course, none of these positive signs has anything much to do with basic Common Market problems such as inflation, paying for oil and whether and how the nine economies should be integrated more closely. Despite all the goodwill there may be in Paris, Brussels and elsewhere, it isn't easy to revive the battered project of European integration. "There's been a change in atmosphere, not so much a change in fact," says one close observer of the Brussels scene.

The difficulties of any relaunching effort were underlined in separate meetings of EC finance and foreign ministers late last month. Brussels officials were counting on finance ministers to make progress on common inflation-fighting programs and on raising funds as a unit in the international marketplace, for use in helping members with serious balance of payments troubles.

But ministers proved to have widely differing ideas on whether they should inflate or deflate their own economies. And West Germany, never anxious to commit its financial resources to its partners without more say in how they run their economies, blocked even agreement in principle on a common borrowing.

The foreign ministers managed to clear the way for a new policy toward Mediterranean nations and for trade-and-aid talks with developing countries. But when it came to a resolution committing the nations to a common energy policy at some future date, they foundered.

Britain's staunchly antimarket trade minister, Peter

Shore, refused to accept a resolution whose consequences he couldn't see. Mr. Shore's attitude startled some officials from other countries, for they hadn't heard any hint of it during preparatory meetings. However, the British ambivalence accurately mirrors the split in the Labour government over remaining in the community.

With Britain questioning its continued membership, West Germany reluctant to shell out more money for European projects and financially-pressed Italy requiring substantial exceptions to EC rules, France has emerged as the community's chief backer. That is a strange turn of events indeed to anyone with even a short memory for the obstructionist tactics of Gaullist days.

But since May [1974] France has had a non-Gaullist president, Valéry Giscard d'Estaing, who is anxious to appear innovative in all fields and finds a convenient outlet for his relatively pro-European ideas in what Paris calls the "relaunching" of the Common Market.

This takes various forms, including dropping long-held opposition to peripheral policies. French representatives have become much more cooperative in the many committees that meet regularly in Brussels, officials from other countries say. Paris has even let it be known that it would join the twelve-nation energy coordination group, so vocally boycotted by Mr. Jobert [predecessor of Mr. Sauvagnargues], if a face-saving formula can be found; this probably will take the form of attaching the group to the Paris-based Organization for Economic Cooperation and Development.

France also accepts the principle of discussing purely political issues, like Cyprus, in the same place as the economic ones, which, strictly speaking, are the only ones the Common Market was founded to cover. Last fall, Mr. Jobert insisted the ministers fly to Copenhagen to talk politics before coming to Brussels the same day for an ordinary EC meeting. But Mr. Sauvagnargues didn't bat an eyelash as he presided over separate political and economic meetings in the same Charlemagne Building here last month. "The

French have improved their manners and that's a good thing," says one Eurocrat.

France's motives don't appear difficult to discern. In cash terms, it is by far the biggest net recipient of funds from the EC budget, so it wouldn't like to see the Common Market collapse completely. And Paris needs to push European cohesion if it is to get backing for the kind of independent foreign policy it cherishes. Such backing won't necessarily come easily from the new leaders of Britain and Germany; both have firmly transatlantic viewpoints.

Mr. Giscard d'Estaing and West German Chancellor Helmut Schmidt are widely believed to have come to an understanding on how to revive the Common Market. But they aren't in any hurry to press their ideas before the British elections expected in October. These elections could alter the European equation by putting the procommunity Conservative party back in office.

Within Britain, debate on Europe increasingly centers on the basic issue of whether to stay in the Common Market or not. Until now—and this is still the government's official view—the aim has been simply to renegotiate the membership terms obtained by the Conservatives. However, these renegotiations are turning out to be a tame affair, which even many Conservatives can support.

As a result, British insiders say, die-hard antimarket ministers are shifting the focus of the debate from the terms of membership to membership itself. Here in Brussels, this debate is being watched with less than keen interest. Planners ponder the community's future without pausing much to consider whether Britain will be a part of it. "The first concern of the Commission is the economy. Britain comes second," says a high official of the Common Market's executive body.

Given Britain's internal politics, any Franco-German relaunching effort can be expected to remain in the background until the fall. The summer vacation period has never been the time for much serious work in Europe anyway. But optimists note that the resolidified Paris-Bonn axis is in sharp contrast to the sniping that emanated from both capitals last summer, when it looked like tough decisions were in the offing and national priorities were in peril.

Two Pragmatic Leaders

However, the tough decisions now have been put off by the perilous international economic climate and both countries are headed by new, pragmatic leaders, both of whom happen to be former finance ministers. Messrs. Schmidt and Giscard d'Estaing know and respect each other from many a conference table, insiders say. The two men don't hesitate to dispense with aides and interpreters to converse in English.

As new leaders, though, each wants to make a quick favorable impression on his home constituency. Mr. Giscard d'Estaing does this by appearing the reformer, Mr. Schmidt by firmly holding the line on spending even to the extent of accepting the resignation of one of his cabinet ministers who objected to the clampdown.

Neither leader would mind a foreign policy initiative under these circumstances. In other Common Market capitals, the expectation is that the initiative will lie in the direction of closer political coordination—on items such as Cyprus, the Middle East and the Atlantic alliance—rather than in an attempt to push the obviously unwilling nations into closer economic alignment.

France previously pushed for a body to coordinate political stands quite separate from the Brussels establishment. At the time, this was seen as an attempt to prevent economic integration from going any further. But with economic integration now in tatters, this may be the time to revive the idea of a political secretariat.

After the recent round of bilateral summits among the leaders of Britain, France and Germany, officials wouldn't be at all surprised to see France bring up the political secretariat again and find support from Mr. Schmidt and British

Prime Minister Harold Wilson. And, some suspect, there might even be agreement to have such a secretariat located outside Brussels, Europe's unofficial capital. The location could be—and some see in this the most fundamental reason of all for France's new sweetness toward its partners—Paris.

But a lot of water would have to flow under the bridge before that could come to pass. A political secretariat would have to be part of a package that included some economic revival. And with so much current economic disarray, it may be all the nine nations can do to preserve what they have left. Most officials figure it will take a good year or two before the international economic scene simmers to the point that the Common Market can return to the way it was a year ago.

Certaintly recent events have shown that it is extremely difficult to get the nine nations to agree to anything new. In these troubled economic times, just keeping the Common Market alive is an accomplishment.

THE COMMUNITY IS WORKING [2]

"Deficit" seems to be the word for Europe these days. The community of the nine, so we are told, has a democratic deficit, a social deficit, a deficit of visionary power and, most noticeably, a deficit of unified political will in world affairs. It is hard to deny that there is a great deal of truth to such jeremiads. The community does indeed find itself in the awkward position of being neither here nor there. Its member states no longer possess a number of important political instruments; collective tools have not yet been fashioned. Clearly, the evolution of joint political institutions has not reached the point where they match the problems in the world.

But if there are glaring deficits in today's Europe, there is also, perhaps, a surfeit of skepticism. For despite all its obvious deficiencies the community is definitely on the move

[2] From article by Theo Sommer, editor-in-chief, *Die Zeit*, Hamburg. *Foreign Affairs*. 51:747-54. Jl. '73. Excerpted by permission from *Foreign Affairs*, July 1973. Copyright 1973 by Council on Foreign Relations, Inc.

again. Europe lost the 1950s through British aloofness, then
the 1960s through French obstinacy. Now the moment of
slack water in the tide of European affairs is obviously past.
The community of the six has finally grown into the wider
grouping of the nine. At the Paris summit last October
[1972], the leaders of the new community made a number
of important decisions about the internal structure of their
association. They defined a long-term poltical goal—European union by 1980—and set themselves a provisional timetable. Whatever procedural snags this renewed effort at pulling together may run into, and whatever vagueness may still
becloud the ultimate objective, the *relance européenne* is
finally underway. If the Treaty of Rome is the community's
Old Testament, the Paris Communiqué is its New Testament. And it goes a long way beyond the earlier document.
Nowhere will this become more clearly visible than in the
community's external relations.

The range of choices has narrowed considerably since
Herman Kahn sketched eighty-eight possible Europes in the
mid-1960s, even since Alastair Buchan's ISS [Institute for
Strategic Studies, London] study of 1969 outlined six different models of thinkable European futures. We may not
see a federated Western Europe emerge by 1980, but we
will see something close to it, arrived at in a much more
pragmatic fashion than the European idealists of the early
postwar period were able to visualize.

There will not be an *American Europe,* the kind of
US-led Western Europe we had in 1949—divided, powerless,
frightened states willingly following American leadership
because it provided the only avenue toward physical survival
—although close links with the United States are no doubt
going to be maintained. Despite the growing prospect of a
more conflictive relationship between the European Community and the United States, there will not be a *Gaullist
Europe,* led by France in the basically anti-American spirit
of Charles de Gaulle—although French influence will doubt-
lessly be significant. A *fragmented Europe*—once more back

to its component parts, its community organs and institutions having come unstuck again—can likewise be rated very improbable. At the same time, a *pan-European evolution* leading to a Europe free from Brest [in France] to Brest [in Russia] does not, in view both of Soviet hegemonial rigidity and the still systemic inability of Communist regimes to cooperate with open societies, constitute a viable or attractive alternative to continued West European integration. Steadfast development of their community to the point of *full-fledged political union* is the only option now open to the nine.

Western Europe's approaches to community building have undergone significant changes in the course of the past twenty years. In fact, there are three clearly distinguishable phases of development, each one characterized by a different approach:

Europe I, originally conceived in the 1950s, was connected with the name of Jean Monnet; its propellant and policy executor was to be the European Commission; its essence was supranational.

Europe II, which France attempted to impose on her partners in the 1960s, is linked with the name of Charles de Gaulle. The driving force behind it was the general's hegemonial ambition for his country; its essence was national, even nationalistic.

Europe III, as it has slowly been evolving, is a different kind of animal. It carries the name tag of Belgian Ambassador Etienne Davignon; its main instrument is the systematic cooperation of governments, leading to the negotiated, agreed-upon extension of collective policies to a rapidly widening range of questions. Its essence is, as it were, transnational.

This Europe III is likely to be with us for some time to come. It will neither be dominated by a technocratic structure nor overwhelmed by one man's autocratic will. It will be a Europe of the possible: pragmatic, without fanfare or panache, but dynamic nevertheless. Joint action will emerge from negotiated communality rather than from agreed Commission plans. But as the nine members formulate collective policies affecting an ever-growing number of sectors, the sheer quantity of joint decisions is bound to change the basic quality of the community. No doubt, its component parts will not disappear, national governments not dwindle into insignificance: they are going to be the constituent parts of tomorrow's Europe as well. Yet in the eyes of the outside world the community will more and more assume the character of one single entity, speaking, although in different tongues, with one voice, and implementing a collective will.

Contrary to earlier expectations, the Commission will not, or not for some time yet, become the main instrument of unity, the chief locus of political imagination and implementation. This may be a disheartening prospect for the Brussels apparatus, but it is not necessarily a disaster so long as the member governments themselves provide the impetus toward more unity. Recent history seems to suggest that this is precisely what is happening. There are limits to the technocratic approach. Real progress toward fusion must rest on the political consent of Europe's component parts; it can be inspired but not assured by the Commission. The main point, as Andrew Shonfield has pointed out, is to "reduce each nation's capacity for making separate decisions without consulting the interests and wishes of its partners in the group." Yet if the frontiers of the nation-state are to be eroded, the nation-states themselves will have to take part in that process by voluntarily surrendering bits of national power. There is no way to circumvent them.

In part, the European Community is already a palpable reality; in part it is still a dream, a hope, an aspiration. The reality is made up of such dreary paper stuff as beef regulations and directives about barbed-wire fences, or shopkeepers' compromises about low-grade wines and cheap onions. But already it is more than that—for one thing because the outside world sees more in it and expects more from it. Close to one hundred states maintain accredited representatives at the Commission headquarters in Brussels. The community has established formalized relations with a number of international bodies like the Organization for Economic Cooperation and Development (OECD), the General Agreement on Tariffs and Trade (GATT), the UN Conference on Trade and Development (UNCTAD) and concluded a score of trade and association agreements with as many different countries. National ministers of the nine traveling abroad have found to their surprise that their interlocutors invariably regard them as European as much as Dutch, French or German ministers.

To be sure, only a small part of the reality encompasses Europe's external relations. These are still basically the prerogative of the member states. As Ralf Dahrendorf, a German commissioner, pointed out in the January 1973 *Round Table:* "There is an almost absurd disproportion between the expectations of Europe's partners in the world, and the instruments which the European Community has at its disposal in order to respond to these expectations." But to do the West Europeans justice, it must be emphasized that during the past few years they have created habits of consultation, cooperation and concentration in many more fields than would have been thought possible even three years ago. And if there was, for a long time, a pitiful shortage of ideas about what the community's place and role in the world ought to be, Europe now stands at "the brink of a moment of creative tension," to borrow a phrase from Italian Commissioner Altiero Spinelli. Slowly the new European idea is taking root. The goals are being defined for tomorrow's community. A sense of togetherness is growing despite all the workaday squabbles about nuts and bolts, chicken feed and oranges.

The summit conference at The Hague (December 1969) and the subsequent Paris summit meeting (October 1972) have set a pattern for progress through negotiated communality of action. At The Hague, the enlargement of the original European Economic Community (EEC) was finally agreed upon. In Paris, European sights were raised to the more distant goal of union by 1980, but at the same time the summiteers laid down a detailed calendar for action. They agreed further to improve political cooperation on foreign policy matters. Foreign ministers will in future meet four times a year instead of twice for this purpose. The aim, as the communiqué put it, is "to deal with problems of current interest and, where possible, to formulate common medium- and long-term positions."

It is easy to sneer that doubling the number of ministerial meetings will not effect any major change in Europe's world role. But as a matter of fact this kind of political cooperation has made considerable headway in recent years. As the Paris Communiqué states, Western Europe is indeed on the road to "establish[ing] its position in world affairs as a distinct entity"—slowly so, sometimes in a rather fumbling fashion, and all too frequently still by declarations rather than by actions. However, there is now an institutionalized process, largely through the Davignon committee, of comparing notes and agreeing on joint language as well as joint lines of approach; this by no means stops short at regular conferences of department chiefs and meetings of their political directors but reaches well down into the middle echelons of the nine foreign offices. On many issues, EEC ambassadors receive joint instructions. EEC ministers conducting talks abroad often personally inform the community ambassadors about their conversations. This is what Chancellor Brandt referred to when he told the London *Times* recently: "Nowadays, in outside countries, in many cases our ambassadors meet. Not too much is said about this in public. . . . Our ambassador saw Gromyko two days ago, and only a few hours after he had reported to his own government he reported to his colleagues from the community."

Beyond this, policy papers define the member states' attitude toward important questions such as the Middle East or the Conference on Security and Cooperation in Europe

(CSCE). Recognition of East Germany, establishment of diplomatic relations with Hanoi, joint reconstruction plans for Vietnam provide further examples of policy coordination among the nine. In this context, the intensive joint preparations for the CSCE preliminary talks in Helsinki have been particularly significant. Not only did the community members harmonize their individual views on both substance and procedure, they also assured the physical presence of the Commission at the talks and agreed that in all matters legally falling within the competence of the community organs, standard EEC procedures must be observed in the formulation of policy statements or decisions. For the rest, there is no denying the fact that a great deal of the community's own work is coming to have important policy implications. The basic positions taken by the nine on such matters as the next GATT round, associated countries and preferential tariff treatment involve central issues in Europe's relationship with the United States, Japan and the Third World.

Thus, Western Europe is on the way toward a joint foreign policy. But its evolution is bound to be slow. Deeply ingrained parochial attitudes will not vanish overnight. Furthermore, even imaginative European leaders find it difficult to visualize Europe's place in the world of the 1980s. The community of the nine is still in search of a role.

It is comparatively easy to define what Europe is *not* going to be like. First, it is hard to imagine that the community will want to become a superpower in the sense in which this term is currently used: a power with global aspirations toward imposing a certain kind of order. Certainly it will have worldwide interests, and must resist any attempt to be relegated to a minor regional league. But I do not envisage European gunboats patrolling the Straits of Malacca, or EEC paratroopers supporting wobbly regimes in faraway countries against rebellious populations. The community will have to have a military capacity to defend its territory but not to exercise its power far from its shores. It will not try to export any particular way of life. It will neither substitute for nor compete with American or Russian efforts to avert or mitigate conflicts in the developing world by direct intervention. Its role could be assertive only where its immediate interests were impinged upon, for example, if its oil supplies from the Middle East were jeopardized.

Second, although the echoes of past glories still reverberate faintly in some quarters, the peoples of the community at large will feel no temptation to resume a colonial role. Europe, whatever its special interests and links with certain neighboring areas, will not be a vehicle for the continuation of colonialism by collective action. The idea that the community might develop into a regional power with its own satellites in the Mediterranean and in Africa is quite preposterous. It may appeal to the systems ideologues of a pentagonal world order in which each of the five dominant powers possesses its private sphere of influence and dependence in the south: the United States in Latin America, Europe in Africa, the Soviet Union on the Indian subcontinent, China in Southeast Asia, Japan in Oceania. But it has little to do with the real world. Europe cannot become a closed bloc, extending from the North Cape to the Cape of Good Hope. It must remain open to partnership with everyone: with North America as well as Eastern Europe, with Asian groupings as well as Latin American countries.

Third, the Europe of 1980 will not simply be a Switzerland cast on a larger scale. To be sure, it is inevitably going to be a community of producers and traders, manufacturing, selling and buying. Yet for its own self-preservation it must actively participate in the web of international organizations from which Switzerland keeps largely aloof. It is not small enough to pass unnoticed—and not big enough to be immune from pressure if it fails to stand up and speak for itself.

But if Europe is not going to be imperialist, colonialist or Helveticized, what then is it going to be like?

First, the European Community has to see to it that it cannot be pushed around by anyone. It must safeguard its existence, its prosperity and its growth potential. On the one hand, the EEC states must seek to prevent *Finlandization*—being swallowed up politically, if not militarily, by the Soviet Union, with only a semblance of autonomy left to them. On the other hand, they have to ward off what might be called *Canadianization*—being pressed into economic subservience to the United States, their autonomy and freedom of choice threatened by dollar diplomacy. Finally, the EEC must resist unfettered activities on the part of US-dominated multinational companies.

Second, beyond these fundamental requisites of self-preservation and self-respect, the community must establish itself as a totally new type of entity—neither parochial nor imperial, neither unassuming nor overbearing—a building block for a broader and more complex international order; a "new intermediary between the national states and the world system," to quote Andrew Shonfield once more. Perhaps, as Jean Monnet has always seen it, it is the beginning of a "process of civilization" whose repercussions extend well beyond community borders. Europe can serve as a model of how to achieve unity despite diversity. It is bound to be a force for openness and liberalism. And it can demonstrate especially to the Third World what Ralf Dahrendorf has termed "cooperation without dependence."

Third, Europe has a moral role to play, and should unabashedly do so. This may strike some as censorious, as in its time did American moralizing. But as Peregrine Worsthorne pointed out in the London *Sunday Telegraph*, it is important that someone act as the conscience of humanity: "The world would be a much poorer place if there were no area which could be relied upon to preach a plausible sermon with some semblance of conviction from a posture of sufficient authority." America, Russia, China, the Third World, Worsthorne suggested, could not fulfill this role. Europe could: "The memory of how we ourselves used to behave badly in the past is too faint to be embarrassing and the likelihood of having to behave as badly in the future too remote to be worrying."

COMMON MARKET DISUNITY [3]

François-Xavier Ortoli, the sad-eyed president of the European Economic Commission, is singing the blues these days over the Common Market he and his fellow Eurocrats administer. Their dream of running a politically unified Western European confederation is foundering. Instead of a union of Europe, they confront, as far as can be seen, an endless vista of sovereign nation-states.

To which any experienced observer of the EEC might say, "So what else is new?" Ortoli is the first Common Market president to quote the French poet Verlaine in private talks, but he is the last in a long line of frustrated Commission leaders running back through Sicco Mansholt to Walter Hallstein.

The current cause of Ortoli's despair is what is seen there as the perfidious French decision to float the franc, to depart from the bloc of currencies clustered around and fixed in relation to the German mark. Ortoli and his predecessors had hoped to force unity among the Common Market's nine members by tying their currencies tightly together. This scheme only reflects the political naiveté and economic unrealism rampant in the EEC's Brussels headquarters.

Several years ago, the Germans tried to tell the Brussels Commission that the Common Market members must first unify their national economic policies, then create a single currency. But the Commission, urged on ironically by the French, would not listen.

The Germans, of course, were right, for both practical and theoretical reasons. Think of the United States. West

[3] From article by Bernard D. Nossiter, London correspondent. Washington *Post*. p A 24. F. 6, '74. Copyright © 1974 by The Washington Post. Reprinted by permission.

Virginia, a poor state, and Illinois, a rich one, enjoy a single currency. Without it, West Virginia would be perpetually in debt to Illinois, provoking the kind of social unrest that arrayed western farmers against eastern bankers and industrialists in the nineteenth century. Or West Virginia would be forced to devalue its currency.

Economists have been telling bureaucrats for some time that no nation can simultaneously enjoy a fixed exchange rate, high employment and the free flow of capital. One of this trio, they say, must give. In the 1930s, nations chose unemployment and the results were cruel and disastrous. Today, no nation will willingly repeat that experience. When the crunch comes, it is the exchange rates that give. . . .

There are equally potent political reasons for regarding the dreams of the Ortolis and Hallsteins as unreal. Western Europe's nations surrendered a measure of sovereignty, of national control, to enter the Common Market. They did so for two principal reasons. They wanted to tie Germany and France so closely together that warfare between them—a catastrophe that tore the continent apart three times in less than a century—would become unthinkable. First the coal and steel community and then the wider economic community achieved precisely this.

The second motivating cause was fear of Soviet expansion. The community's founders thought that an economic customs union would lead inevitably to a political union, and this was necessary to hold off the scores of Soviet divisions poised at the borders.

The Soviet divisions are still there. But it is hard to convince many in Western Europe that they are likely to roll across the German plain. NATO [North Atlantic Treaty Organization], nuclear weaponry and détente have turned the Russians into a distant potential rather than a pressing actual threat.

Deprived of this fear, the Common Market's members have understandably lost the will to make further surrenders of sovereignty, most notably and recently over obstacles to their unilateral scramble for oil. For a time, Brussels, aided by the French, tried to promote the United States as a substitute villain, particularly large American multinational corporations. But this approach could not succeed. The so-called technology gap disappeared in the American payments deficit. More important, the United States provides Europe with its nuclear shield.

Does this then spell the end of the Common Market? There is no reason to think so and every reason to believe that it will continue more or less as it has, as a customs union and farm price support policy among sovereign states.

Free trade and a common external tariff are eminently suited to German industry and large corporations in the other member states. The nearly free movement of capital pleases London. The price support policy enriches farmers in France, Holland, Denmark and Ireland. There is, in short, something for everybody, even in a community with more modest political ambitions.

Or almost everybody. The British, with some reason, think this arrangement does less for them than anybody else. Prime Minister Edward Heath drove Britain into the community last year despite the misgivings of a majority of the population. He did so in the hope that it would give a Britain stripped of empire a new role, leader of a politically potent bloc.

But now that the community is again seen for what it really is, a convenient commercial arrangement among some continental states, Heath's reason for entry is disappearing.

Opposition to the community reaches new heights in every [British] opinion poll. . . . Even in the foreign office, that rock of support for British membership, heretical mutterings can now be heard. If the community does not develop more cohesion, officials say, we could look without dismay on a Labour government that would weaken the tie.

None of this will please Ortoli and his Brussels colleagues. But their ambitions do not necessarily coincide with even the general, let alone the national good. Unity is a splendid word. When it is based on political and economic unwisdom it is only rhetoric.

LIVING ON CRISES [4]

What I have just said about the difficulties with which the community is faced should not mislead us into believing that the community has no future. It has a future. But there are no panaceas for it.

When I said that the community lived on crises, this meant that, ultimately, crises always act as catalysts of further development. But, of course, we should not just sit back and wait for something to happen, for crises do not pass of their own accord. They are a challenge to us to take decisions.

To my mind, integration can progress relatively easily in the classical sphere of the treasury, that is, in shaping and administering the community budget.

You will agree: It has never been possible to judge the community by the standard of run-of-the-mill international organizations. Its aim and object has always gone beyond that of a mere international utility maintained by the contributions of its user-members. From the start, the European Community was set to become a new—and in the end supranational—level of political organization. It was clear, therefore, that some day this new political entity would dispose of its own financial resources.

At present, we are in the middle of the change from the original system of members' financial contributions to the new one of independent resources. By 1975, all receipts from the variable levies on agricultural imports from third countries and from common tariff customs duties will be community revenue; to this will be added a growing share—not exceeding 1 percent of a uniform assessment base—of na-

[4] From "Europe Is Alive but Living on Crises," address delivered at the Institute for International Affairs, London, January 29, 1974, by Chancellor Helmut Schmidt of West Germany (then minister of finance). Text from *Vital Speeches of the Day*. 40:329-30. Mr. 15, '74.

tional value added tax receipts. (I will concede that neither this assessment base nor the exact amount within the 1 percent limit has so far been agreed upon or even elaborated.)

But anyway, this means that the community's resources have limits. For another, the communities' resources are cycle-related since they depend on business activity through value added tax.

This built-in limited buoyancy of receipts may be assumed to swell the community's purse each year. What is done with the money should now come under closer political and financial control. For it profoundly affects public finance and government responsibilities down to the most humble level. . . .

Closer control of community finance will initially have to be the responsibility of the Council of Ministers. I feel, though, that it will also be necessary to enlarge the apparatus of the Commission by appointing a financial controller. . . .

Furthermore, we consider it inescapable that the powers of the European Parliament as the organ of democracy in the community should be strengthened. As far as I am concerned this means that it should be involved in the decision-making process at every stage. This is the only way to give that which is happening in Europe in this day and age the proper seal of democratic legitimacy.

I hope that these lines of thinking will help to create a sounder financial setup for the European Community and that this will assist us in coming to terms with the objects of common European policy.

And as far as these are concerned—and I have no illusions in this respect—there is still much to be done even if, in view of past experience, we were to allow ourselves a little more time for the process.

But European policy makers will continue to be called upon to ensure the evolution of the peoples of this continent within the framework of a common political system. Moreover, the most recent problems affecting all of us—the fuel crisis and the condition of the international monetary system—call for a coordinated independent contribution by us Europeans and not merely for lone moves by the French, the British or the Germans. The oil supply crisis and the fantastic increase in oil prices can very soon shake the very foundations of the international division of labor: balances of payment, exchange rates and international trade. The Third World's developing countries are at least as badly hit as the industrial world. The danger of enormous deficits on current accounts leads me again to a very urgent warning against sparking off a devaluation race or against introducing trade restrictions. This is the very time when we should not seek refuge in isolationist action.

If Europe wants to have a decisive word to say in international politics in between the United States and the USSR, the superpowers, and the emerging power center, China, it must come to terms on common policies. The offer to cooperate and to reach equitable compromises in dealings with the outside world will be more convincing if it reflects a similar behavior in dealings within the community.

Among members of the European Community there is certainly no argument about the fact that there is no other alternative to Europe. But this conviction is of not much use unless we stop asking what Europe can do for us and instead ask what we can do for Europe.

"LET ONE HUNDRED FLOWERS BLOOM" [5]

Professor Ralf Dahrendorf of West Germany is the first commissioner of the European Community to head a separate department of research, science, and education. [He left that post in 1974 for the London School of Economics.— Ed.] The new department was created when the Commission was enlarged and reorganized after Britain, Denmark, and Ireland joined the community at the beginning of 1973.

[5] From "In a Hard Year in Brussels, Things Look Up for Science," by John Walsh, head, news staff. *Science.* 184:962-3. My. 31, '74. Copyright 1974 by the American Association for the Advancement of Science. Reprinted by permission.

Dahrendorf's transfer from responsibility for external relations—a major job on the Commission—was regarded as an
institutional put-down for a maverick. Now it seems generally agreed that Dahrendorf has done a good job with an
unpromising portfolio, and there is some concern that the
momentum established might not be maintained when
Dahrendorf leaves Brussels next autumn [1974] to become
director of the London School of Economics (LSE).

Dahrendorf has been something of a controversial figure
in the community executive, particularly in the period following his appointment in 1970. In West Germany he combined an academic career, most recently as professor of
sociology at the University of Konstanz, with activity in state
and national politics as a member of the Free Democrat
party. The FDP is the small, non-Socialist, "reform" party,
which provides the parliamentary voting margin in West
Germany's governing coalition dominated by the Social
Democrats. Dahrendorf had acquired a reputation for out-
spokenness by the time he became parliamentary under-
secretary of the West German foreign minister, and it has
been suggested that this quality may have hastened his as-
signment to Brussels.

In Brussels, Dahrendorf generated a tempest through an
article in the German weekly *Die Zeit,* which attracted wide
notice in the European press because of its barbed criticism
of the Eurocrats of Brussels. The article appeared under a
pseudonym, but Dahrendorf was soon identified as the
writer. Dahrendorf remained cheerfully unrepentant under
a sharp reaction that included calls for his resignation and
direct attacks on the floor of the European Parliament.

While his characterization of the community executive
of five thousand as a "bureaucratic leviathan" entangled in
red tape drew the headlines, it was his questioning of pre-
vailing assumptions about progress toward European political unification which probably accounted for the harshness
of the reactions of some of his colleagues in the Brussels
establishment.

In essence, Dahrendorf rejected the idea that member governments of the community in the foreseeable future will agree to give up significant elements of sovereignty to a "federal" European government. He sees political unification in Europe evolving only after the member states of the community further strengthen the web of relationships already begun, so that national interests eventually converge. He argued that a Europe of the "second generation" must undertake this task.

Dahrendorf has not changed his mind. In an interview in late April Dahrendorf said the community has reached "an impasse in its calendar for progress." For a decade before 1972 "people had a notion [that the community would] proceed from the customs plan through economic and monetary union to something described as political union, a royal way planned in stages," said Dahrendorf.

"When I said impasse, I meant the end of a chapter, a chapter in which a calendar devised by community institutions was imposed on reality. Well, reality has caught up with us. Reality has told us we are not where we planned to be."

The way to European union, says Dahrendorf, is not by devising a comprehensive calendar, a royal way. Rather he says he is in favor of the Maoist line of "letting a hundred flowers bloom."

"What we have to do, in fact, is to solve a large number of specific problems, build up the materials for European union." He believes that the area he is responsible for is peculiarly suited to this pursuit; it provides "varied leads to real results." And with touches of both the self-confidence and self-inclusive irony that are characteristic of him, he says, "I have constructed for myself a portfolio necessary in the community."

Dahrendorf, who is in his middle forties, might himself be described as a European of the second generation with experience and expectations quite different from those of many of his older colleagues in the Commission and in the higher reaches of the community apparatus. For example, Altiero Spinelli, of Italy, who, before expansion of the Commission, was the commissioner responsible for many of the programs and policies now in Dahrendorf's province, is a strong advocate of political integration under a federal system. Spinelli spent sixteen years in detention in Fascist Italy, ten of them actually in prison after, as a student, he was first arrested for political activity in 1927. He became identified with the European federalist movement almost immediately after he was freed in 1943, and he pursued that interest in parallel with academic and literary and political activity in postwar Italy. He joined the Commission in 1970 as commissioner responsible for science, technology, and industry and, since the expansion of the Commission, has been responsible for industry and technology. He remains a powerful advocate of common policies in the fields he oversees, regarding them as prerequisites and aids to political unification. The Council of Ministers, which decides on policy proposals made by the Commission, largely rejected Spinelli's ideas in this area, although, ironically, many of the proposals included in the science policy program, finally accepted this year, originated with Spinelli.

TOWARDS A EUROPEAN GOVERNMENT [6]

I appear before you at a time when serious doubt, even a feeling of resignation and defeat, is weighing heavily upon the entire European venture. This could well turn out to be one of the many political ventures that break down before being fully realized, because the effort of will, the imaginative force and the political insight of those responsible for undertaking them flag. As a member of the Commission of the European communities, an institution which is in the

[6] Excerpts from address by Altiero Spinelli, European Community commissioner responsible for industrial policy, accepting the 1974 Robert Schuman Prize at the Rheinische Friedrich-Wilhelm University, Bonn, Germany, March 12, 1974. (Document CAB/VII/137/74-E) European Community Information Service. 2100 M Street, N.W. Washington, D.C. 20037. '74.

forefront of the European venture, I am one of those who bear this responsibility. If the European venture were to fail, the whole past history of men and institutions would be of very little consequence to you and future generations. . . .

For some years now the course of events has not been kind to Europe, especially in the last year. The only successes have been the accession of three new members to the community, and the fact that all the states of black Africa, without exception, have sought to open general negotiations for association with the community. Apart from these two positive points, there have been only defeats and setbacks. . . .

Parliament

Among all the institutions of the European Community, the parliament, which is the most independent of government choices, has always been the one most capable of developing transnational groupings of political forces, the most impregnated with European spirit and the most decided when it comes to demanding limitations on national sovereignties and . . . [fostering supranational] developments. And, with the passing of the years, this trend has continued to become stronger, while it was weakening in the other institutions. It has gone on gathering strength on the right and on the left, where initially it was weakest: in the European democratic group and in the Communist group.

I said [political inertia would disappear] "if the political forces were to participate." The fact is that hitherto they have always been excluded from any direct and real participation in the construction of Europe. This lack of democratic participation is the deep-seated and ultimate reason for the present powerlessness, and until it is corrected this initial defect will paralyze the process of building Europe and renationalizing will continue.

The defect is really an initial one and has never been

corrected so far. Monnet, Schuman, and the other statesmen who answered their call, well understood that the profound meaning of their initiative resided entirely in a simple and strong idea: If different states wish to pool certain matters on a permanent basis, they must transfer certain competences to a common authority distinct from that of the states.

Between 1951 and 1953 the great European ministers explored this idea and arrived at its logical conclusion: It was not sufficient to build specialized authorities but a political community had to be set up, i.e. a European government democratically controlled by the European people and by representatives of the member states.

Having then met with strong political resistance, they fell back on what we are wont to call a pragmatic solution, that is to say an incoherent one, and created a community in which what should have been common was defined, but the common authority distinct from the governments received only the power to propose what should be done, while the power to decide remained in the hands of the representatives of the individual governments meeting in the council.

This was perhaps all that could be achieved at the time. But what was born in this way was born to be doomed in the medium term. The Europe of offices was born, the Europe of secret sessions, the Europe of perpetual intergovernmental negotiation, the Europe of the refusal of democratic participation, the Europe in which, admittedly, a European Parliament was set up but one which was refused any real power and in which even the undertaking to have it elected directly was suddenly forgotten.

It is a strange thing to say that the community's greatest success was precisely the one which it had not aimed at achieving: It has contributed, by the mere fact of its existence, to spreading the idea that united Europe is a reality in the course of construction and that this construction has to be promoted. Europe has thus become a permanent constituent datum, even if still a confused one, in the popular mind of the six original member countries and has then led three other countries to join.

On the other hand its greatest failure has been its own functioning. "To hope"—Hamilton wrote about two centuries ago—"for the maintenance of harmony between several and neighboring states would be to lose sight of the uniform course of human events and to go against the experience of the centuries." The community was founded on this hope and the result has been that foreseen by Hamilton.

As long as it was a matter of carrying out common commitments already defined and accepted in the treaties, an intergovernmental conference such as the council is, was still capable of listening to the Commission and getting things moving. But when joint-action programs had to be formulated in new fields and then approved, implemented, adapted to changing reality, modified and even abolished and replaced by others, the machinery proved to be powerless by nature and every appeal to political will turned into superficial rhetoric. . . .

The downgrading of the Commission, the refusal of democratic participation, the secrecy of negotiations in the council, and the final paralysis, are the inevitable consequences of a system in which there is no real balance between the national interests and the interests of the community as such. All the real powers have been allocated to the national governments, even those that they are unable to exercise, and all the real powers have been refused to the community, even those which it alone could and should exercise. . . .

The substance of a real new takeoff for Europe today is implicit in the analysis I have made of the community's illness. We must decide to bring about the immediate and genuine participation of all the political forces in the construction of Europe. The moment has come to bring European democracy to birth. . . .

To will a European government will mean drawing up and ratifying a treaty containing the constitution of such a government and of the other institutions which must complete it. Such a treaty-constitution once framed will have to be submitted to the parliaments or to national referendums for ratification, since it is only in this way that it will be possible to decide on transfers of powers from the national level to that of the union. But who should draw up the treaty and approve it before it is ratified? . . .

This cannot happen in any other way than by entrusting the mandate to draw up the draft treaty to the only European institution in which all the political forces are really represented, that is to say the European Parliament. . . .

We should not tire of repeating that the current decomposition of Europe is not due to a rebirth of nationalistic feelings. It is due to political machinery which allows only national trends to express themselves and clips the wings of those European trends which however less still exist and are vigorous. This decomposition is for this reason accompanied by a bad conscience and fear for the future. New ideas, efforts of imagination, acts of courage usually emerge in such circumstances and not when everything is plain sailing. For all those who are attached to the future of Europe it is therefore a matter of concentrating their action in such a way that the scandal of a Europe which should and can emerge and which, nonetheless, is in the process of destroying itself may become intolerable.

President [Jean] Rey recently said that in Europe we have reached the day of anger. I hope that this address of mine may be my contribution to stirring up this anger and, at the same time, my sober contribution to indicating that the road of salvation exists for Europe and that in any case it is not so very difficult to follow it.

BIBLIOGRAPHY

An asterisk (*) preceding a reference indicates that the article or a part of it has been reprinted in this book.

BOOKS, PAMPHLETS, AND DOCUMENTS

Andrews, Stanley. Agriculture and the Common Market. Iowa State University Press. '73.

Bottcher, Winfried and others. Great Britain and Europe 1940-1970. Droste Verlag. '71.

Bouvard, Marguerite. Labor movements in the Common Market countries: the growth of a European pressure group. Praeger. '72.

Broad, Roger and Jarrett, R. J. Community Europe today. rev & enl ed. Wolff. '72.

Commission of the European Communities. The Common Agricultural Policy. rev. European Community Information Service. 2100 M St. N.W. Washington, D.C. 20037. '73.

*Commission of the European Communities. European Community: the facts. European Community Information Service. 2100 M St. N.W. Washington, D.C. 20037. '72.

Commission of the European Communities. Uniting Europe: the European Community since 1950. European Community Information Service. 2100 M St. N.W. Washington, D.C. 20037. '72.

Committee for Economic Development. The United States and the European Community: policies for a changing world economy. The Committee. 477 Madison Ave. New York 10022. '71.

Coombes, David and Wiebecke, Ilka. The power of the purse in European communities. Chatham House. '72.

Cosgrove, C. A. A readers guide to Britain and the European communities. Political and Economic Planning (P.E.P.). 12 Upper Belgrave St. London S.W. 1. '73.

Davis, Ralph. The rise of the Atlantic economies. Cornell University Press. '73.

Diebold, William, Jr. The United States and the industrial world: American foreign economic policy in the 1970s. Praeger. '72.

Dinwiddy, Bruce, ed. Aid performance and development policies of Western countries: studies in US, UK, EEC and Dutch programs. Praeger [in association with the Overseas Development Institute]. '73.

Einzig, Paul. The case against joining the Common Market. St. Martins. '71.

European Communities Commission. Memorandum agriculture 1973-1978. (Special issue, Newsletter on the Common Agricultural Policy) Directorate-General for Agriculture. European Communities Commission. 200 rue de la Loi. Brussels. '73.

European Community Information Service. The energy crisis and the European Community. (Background Note no 5) The Service. 2100 M St. N.W. Washington, D.C. 20037. '74.

European Community Information Service. Multinational corporations: problems confronting Europe. (European Studies 16) The Service. 2100 M St. N.W. Washington, D.C. 20037. '73.

European Community Information Service. Questions and answers about the European Community. rev. Manhattan Publishing Company. '73.

European Community Information Service. A selective study guide to the European communities. The Service. 2100 M St. N.W. Washington, D.C. 20037. '73.

European Community Information Service. The United States and the European Community: their common interests. 2d ed. rev. Manhattan Publishing Company. '73.

European Community Information Service. United States policy towards postwar Western Europe. (European Studies, Teacher's Series no 17) The Service. 2100 M St. N.W. Washington, D.C. 20037. '73.

European Parliament. Secretariat. The European Parliament. Directorate-General for Information and Public Relations. P.O. Box 1601. Luxembourg. '73.

European Parliament. Secretariat. Report on European political cooperation and unification. (Working Document no 12/73) rev. Directorate-General for Information and Public Relations. P.O. Box 1601. Luxembourg. '73.

Farnsworth, C. H. Out of this nettle: a history of postwar Europe. John Day. '73.

*Foreign Policy Association. Great decisions 1973. The Association. 345 E. 46th St. New York 10017. '73.

    Reprinted in this volume: Topic no 5. The Common Market expands: can the U.S. compete? p 51-2, 54-6.

*France, Boyd. A short chronicle of United States-European Community relations. European Community Information Service. 2100 M St. N.W. Washington, D.C. 20037. '73.

Galtung, Johan. The European Community: a superpower in the making. G. Allen. '73.

Gasteyger, Curt. Europe and America at the crossroads. Atlantic Institute for International Affairs. 120 rue de Longchamps. Paris 16. '72.

Geiger. Theodore. The fortunes of the West: the future of the Atlantic nations. Indiana University Press. '73.

Haferkamp, Wilhelm. Prospects for monetary integration in the EC; address before German bankers' convention, Bonn, Germany, March 12, 1974. European Community Information Service. 2100 M St. N.W. Washington, D.C. 20037. '74.

Hallstein, Walter. Europe in the making; tr. by Charles Roetter. Norton. '73.

Hennessy, James, comp. Britain and Europe since 1945; a bibliographical guide: an author, title and chronological index to British primary source material on European integration issued since 1945. Harvester Press. '73.

Hodges, Michael. European integration; selected readings. Penguin. '72.

Ionescu, Ghita, ed. The new politics of European integration. St. Martins. '72.

Jones, David. Europe's chosen few: policy and practice of the EEC aid programme. Overseas Development Institute Ltd. 160 Piccadilly. London WIV OJS. '73.

Kaiser, Karl. Europe and the United States: the future of the relationship. Columbia Books. '73.

Kindleberger, C. P. and Shonfield, Andrew, eds. North American and Western European economic policies; proceedings of a conference held by the International Economic Association. St. Martins; Macmillan (London). '71.

*Kissinger, H. A. 1973: the Year of Europe; address before annual meeting of Associated Press editors, New York, N.Y., April 23, 1974. (Department of State Publication 8710) Supt. of Docs. Washington, D.C. 20402. '73.
    Same. Department of State Bulletin. 68:593-8. My. 14, '73.

Kitzinger, Uwe. Diplomacy and persuasion: how Britain joined the Common Market. Thames (London). '73.

Knorr, Klaus. The Atlantic alliance: a reappraisal. (Headline Series no 221) Foreign Policy Association. 345 E. 46th St. New York 10017. '74.

Knox, Francis. The Common Market and world agriculture; trade patterns in temperate-zone foodstuffs. Pall Mall. '72.

Kohnstamm, Max and Hager, Wolfgang, eds. A nation writ large? foreign-policy problems before the European Community. Wiley. '73.

Krause, L. B. and Salant, W. S. European monetary unification and its meaning for the United States. Brookings. '73.
Conference on the Implications of European Monetary Integration for the United States, 1972; papers by A. I. Bloomfield and others.

Korbel, Josef. Détente in Europe; real or imaginary? Princeton University Press. '72.

Lindberg, L. N. and Scheingold, S. A. Europe's would-be policy. Prentice-Hall. '70.
Review article: International Organization. 27:225-54. Spring '73. Euro-European integration: forward march, parade rest, or dismissed? R. D. Hansen.

Lindberg, L. N. and Scheingold, S. A. Regional integration, theory and research. Harvard University Press. '71.
Review article: International Organization. 27:225-54. Spring '73. European integration: forward march, parade rest, or dismissed? R. D. Hansen.

McLin, Jon. European Community and the Mediterranean: co-prosperity sphere or North-South confrontation zone? (West Europe Series, v 8 no 2) American Universities Field Staff. Box 150. Hanover, N.H. 03755. '73.

McLin, Jon. Europe's Common Agricultural Policy in a time of shortages. (West Europe Series, v 8 no 10) American Universities Field Staff. Box 150. Hanover, N.H. 03755. '73.

McLin, Jon. A note on the European Community: 1973. (West Europe Series, v 8 no 3) American Universities Field Staff. Box 150. Hanover, N.H. 03755. '73.

Magnifico, Giovanni. European monetary unification. Wiley. '73.

Mally, Gerhard. The European Community in perspective: the new Europe, the United States, and the world. Heath. '73.

Mayne, Richard. The Europeans: who are we? Library Press; Weidenfeld. '72.

Mayne, Richard. The recovery of Europe, 1945-1973. rev. Doubleday. '73.

Milward, A. S. and Saul, S. B. The economic development of continental Europe: v 1, 1780-1870. Rowman & Littlefield. '73.

Morgan, Roger. West European politics since 1945: the shaping of the European Community. Batsford. '72.

Mowat, R. C. Creating the European Community. Harper. '73.

Nader, Ralph and others, eds. Whistle blowing; the report of the Conference on Professional Responsibility, Washington, D.C., 1971. Grossman. '72.

*Noël, Emile. How the European Community's institutions work. (Community Topics, 39) rev. ed. European Community Information Office. 2100 M St. N.W. Washington, D.C. 20037. '73.

Preeg, E. H. Economic blocs and U.S. foreign policy. (NPA Report no 135) National Planning Association. 1606 New Hampshire Ave. Washington, D.C. 20009. '74.

Pryce, Roy. The politics of the European Community. Rowman & Littlefield. '73.

Ransom, Charles. The European Community and Eastern Europe. Rowman & Littlefield. '73.

Servan-Schreiber, J. J. The American challenge. Atheneum. '68.

Shonfield, Andrew. Europe—journey to an unknown destination; an expanded version of the BBC Reith Lectures. Allen Lane. '73.

    Review article: Political Studies. 21:376-9. S. '73. The political study of the European Community. Ghita Ionescu.

Silberschmidt, Max. The United States and Europe: rivals and partners. Harcourt. '72.

Soames, Sir Christopher. Britain in the Common Market; address before Cunard International, London, May 2, 1974. European Community Information Service. 2100 M Street. N.W. Washington, D.C. 20037. mimeo.

Spaak, P. H. The continuing battle: memoirs of a European, 1936-1966. Weidenfeld. '71.

*Spinelli, Altiero. Address accepting the 1974 Robert Schuman Prize, Rheinische Friedrich-Wilhelm University, Bonn, Germany, March 12, 1974. (Document CAB/VII/137/74-E) European Community Information Service. 2100 M St. N.W. Washington, D.C. 20037. '74.

Thomas, Hugh. Europe, the radical challenge. Harper. '73.

Tulloch, Peter. The seven outside: Commonwealth Asia's trade with the enlarged EEC. Overseas Development Institute Ltd. 160 Piccadilly. London. WIV OJS. '73.

United States. Congress. House. Committee on Foreign Affairs. Subcommittee on Foreign Economic Policy. New realities and new directions in United States foreign economic policy; a report. 92d Congress, 2d session. Supt. of Docs. Washington, D.C. 20402. '72.

United States. Congress. House. Special Study Mission to Europe. The European Community and the American interest; report by Benjamin S. Rosenthal and Donald M. Fraser, Committee on Foreign Affairs, pursuant to H. Res. 109. 92d Congress, 2d session. U.S. Gov. Ptg. Off., Washington, D.C. 20401. '72.

Uri, Pierre. L'Europe se gaspille. Hachette. '73.

Wallace, Helen. National governments and the European communities. Chatham House. '73.

Walsh, A. E. and Paxton, John. Into Europe: the structure and development of the Common Market. 2d ed. Hutchinson. '72.

Warnecke, S. J. ed. The European Community in the 1970s. Praeger. '72.

Periodicals

America. 128:138-9. F. 17, '73. Europe has a parliament; P. M. Kirk's proposals. Peter Hebblethwaite.

Atlantic. 231:18+. F. '73. Common Market. Don Cook.

Atlantic Community Quarterly. 10:215-25. Summer '72. The enlargement of the European Community and Atlantic relations: economic and monetary implications. W. J. Feld.

Atlantic Community Quarterly. 11:79-92. Spring '73. Economic relations across the Atlantic: an agenda for cooperation. Giovanni Agnelli.

Business Week. p 66. Ap. 28, '73. EEC: protectionism is the trade hurdle.

Business Week. p 37. D. 1, '73. Europe: the EC [European Community] feud over nuclear fuel.

Business week. p 51+. D. 8, '73. Netherlands: oil holds the key to European unity.

Business Week. p 27. Ap. 6, '74. Real threat to European unity.

Commentary. 55:74-80. Je. '73. Year of Europe. Walter Laqueur.

Commentary. 57:27-35. Ap. '74. End of the postwar era. Fritz Stern.

Contemporary Review. 222:184-7. Ap. '73. The economic situation in the Community at the beginning of 1973. Wilhelm Haferkamp.

Contemporary Review. 223:169-73. O. '73. The European Parliament. James Scott-Hopkins.

Current. 148:35-9. F. '73. New European super-power? David Astor.

Current. 148:39-41. F. '73. Where will power lie in the Community? Andrew Shonfield.

Current History. 64:145-77+. Ap. '73. Western Europe, 1973; symposium.

Current History. 66:111-15+. Mr. '74. Britain and Europe: a new relationship? R. H. Leach.

Department of State Bulletin. 66:198. F. 14, '72. U.S. welcomes signing of treaty to enlarge European Community; statement, January 22, 1972.

Department of State Bulletin. 66:515-17. Ap. 3, '72. U.S. and European Community agree on trade measures; text of U.S.-European Community declaration, with texts of letters, February 11, 1972. T. C. Hijzen; W. D. Eberle.

Department of State Bulletin. 68:539-43. Ap. 30, '73. U.S. policy toward the European Community; statement, April 5, 1973. W. J. Casey.

Department of State Bulletin. 68:593-8. My. 14, '73. Year of Europe; address, April 23, 1973. H. A. Kissinger.

Department of State Bulletin. 69:777-82. D. 31, '73. The United States and a unifying Europe: the necessity for partnership; address delivered before the Pilgrims of Great Britain, London, December 12, 1973. H. A. Kissinger.

Department of State Bulletin. 70:237-41. Mr. 11, '74. European-American relations: a case for cooperative endeavor; address, February 15, 1974. Kenneth Rush.

Department of State Bulletin. 70:284-5. Mr. 18, '74. International economic report transmitted to the Congress; February 7, 1974. R. M. Nixon.

Department of State Bulletin. 70:353-61. Ap. 8, '74. Secretary Kissinger's news conference, March 21, 1974. H. A. Kissinger.

Dun's. 101:69-71+. Ap. '73. Is Britain ready for Europe? Jean Ross-Skinner.

Dun's. 102:84-5+. N. '73. What's ahead for the multinationals in Europe? Jean Ross-Skinner.

*Economist. 242:52-3. Ja. 22, '72. Who's afraid of the European Commission?

Economist. 247:53-4. Je. 30, '73. Farm policy's all wrong: here's—er—how we put it right.

Economist. 248:57. Jl. 21, '73. Accountants: six and three become one.

Economist. 248:70+. S. 22, '73. European Parliament: Strasbourg's a bore.

Economist. 249:69-70. O. 13, '73. Must Strasbourg's members stay *castrati* for ever?

Economist. 249:80-1. O. 27, '73. Time the European bus had a thorough overhaul.

Economist. 249:77. N. 3, '73. Monetary union; Europe by many stages.

Economist. 249:72. N. 17, '73. Monetary union; Eurotick.

Economist. 249:74. N. 17, '73. Multinationals; nothing to fear yet.

Economist. 249:61-2. D. 15, '73. The sorcerer and his European apprentice.

Economist. 251:65. Ap. 20, '74. But Irish eyes still smile on Brussels.

*Economist. 251:66. Ap. 20, '74. Then there were seven?

Economist. 251:71. My. 4, '74. Half way up the meat mountain Italy sits down.

Economist. 251:76+. My. 4, '74. Will Labour be trapped or saved by the state aid web?

Economist. 251:92-3. My. 4, '74. France: the economic issues.

Economist. 251:56. My. 18, '74. Denmark's formidable Finn.

Economist. 251:59. My. 18, '74. The nine Muses sing the blues.

*Economist. 251:14-15. Je. 1, '74. The trimline new Europe.

Economist. 251:60+. Je. 1, '74. Britain: Oliver Twist's homework.
*Economist. 251:66-7. Je. 1, '74. EEC: the British shopping list.
Economist. 251:41-2. Je. 15, '74. Will falling prices boomerang against the pro-marketeers?
Economist. 252:59-60. Jl. 6, '74. The economies: Gladstone's still in charge.
Economist. 252:63. Jl. 6, '74. Beef: a massive beef surplus in store?
European Community. 162:3. Ja. '73. When six became nine.
European Community. 162:4-5. Ja. '73. The "nine" join destinies.
European Community. 162:6-7. Ja. '73. Plus or minus for the United States?
European Community. 162:8-9. Ja. '73. United Kingdom: Britain bridges the Channel.
European Community. 162:10-11. Ja. '73. Ireland: the emerald isle goes European.
European Community. 162:12-13. Ja. '73. Denmark: a Nordic contribution.
*European Community. 164:8-11. Ap. '73. Power: society's most consumed product. John Nielsen.
European Community. 164:19-21. Ap. '73. Yaounde III: an African strategy. R. K. A. Gardiner.
European Community. 166:6-9. Je. '73. Speaking out on trade and aid. Christopher Soames.
European Community. 166:10-11. Je. '73. Clouds over the Atlantic. Flora Lewis.
European Community. 166:12-14. Je. '73. European law: a growing force. Jean LeCerf.
European Community. 166:17-19. Je. '73. Latin America and Europe: an evolving dialogue. Betsy Baker.
European Community. 166:20-1. Je. '73. Could Europe elect a parliament? Richard Rose.
*European Community. 167:8-9. Jl. '73. How Americans rate the European Community.
European Community. 167:13-14. Jl. '73. U.S. policy toward Europe. L. B. Tennyson.
European Community. 167:15-17. Jl. '73. "Year of Europe": a mid-year report. David Fouquet.
European Community. 167:20-2. Jl. '73. Partnership, not association: Yaounde convention to be replaced.
European Community. 169:7. O. '73. How common is common?
European Community. 169:8-10. O. '73. Cambrinus reports: the story of beer in the European Community. W. J. Reckman.
European Community. 169:17-18. O. '73. Dialogue not dispute. Pierre Uri.

European Community. 170:15-17. N. '73. GATT talks begin. Mary
  Locke and Hans Binnedijk.
European Community. 170:18-20. N. '73. The East looks West.
  Gerald Segal.
European Community. 171:7-11. D. '73. Europe's working women:
  EC Commission finds pay bias.
European Community. 171:20-2. D. '73. Britain's second thoughts.
  M. U. Mauthner.
*European Community. 172:8-10. Ja. '74. "Year of Europe" I: re-
  flections on the year that was (not). Peter Jenkins.
European Community. 172:11-12. Ja. '74. "Year of Europe" II.
  Barbara Bright-Sagnier.
European Community. 172:13-16. Ja. '74. A call for European
  unity. Willy Brandt.
*European Community. 173:6-8. F. '74. First "fireside summit."
European Community. 173:9-13. F. '74. Chronology of a crisis:
  energy shortage hits Europe. Vincent Roberts.
European Community. 173:19-22. F. '74. Whither multinationals?
  Commission proposes common EC.
*European Community. 174:11-12. Mr. '74. Speaking out on US-
  EC relations: to be an equal partner, Europe must unite. Sir
  Christopher Soames.
    Abridgment of address delivered to the European Parliament, January
  16, 1974.
European Community. 174:13-16. Mr. '74. The politics of energy:
  crisis affects EC solidarity and US-EC relations. M. U. Mauth-
  ner.
European Community. 175:8-10. Ap. '74. Conference and crisis.
  Emanuele Gazzo.
European Community. 175:11. Ap. '74. Conference notebook. Ed-
  ward Cowan.
European Community. 175:12-14. Ap. '74. "State of the Com-
  munity." F. X. Ortoli.
European Community. 176:11-12. My. '74. Puzzling over US-EC
  relations. J. O. Krag.
European Community. 176:13-15. My. '74. Atlantic squalls: recent
  US-EC differences are part of changing international "club"
  life. David Binder.
European Community. 176:16-17. My. '74. Crisis politics. R. C.
  Longworth.
European Community. 177:10-11. Je. '74. Prospects for economic
  and monetary union. John Pinder.
European Community. 177:12-13. Je. '74. Economic woes; EC
  Commission calls for austerity. Ferdinando Riccardi.

European Community. 177:14-16. Je. '74. Transatlantic turmoil. H. P. Dreyer.

European Community. 178:12-13. Jl. '74. Shifting mood and system. Z. K. Brzezinski.

European Community. 178:14-16. Jl. '74. Bretton Woods: 30. Vincent Roberts.

European Community. 178:17-18. Jl. '74. New leaders, a new Europe? Emanuele Gazzo.

*European Community. 178:19-22. Jl. '74. New leaders, a new Atlantic alliance? J. G. Reifenberg.

Forbes. 113:112-14. My. 15, '74. Europe likes them big; new guidelines for mergers in the European Common Market.

Foreign Affairs. 51:353-66. Ja. '73. Western Europe: stuck fast. John Newhouse.

Foreign Affairs. 51:367-79. Ja. '73. Western Europe: why the malaise? E. L. Morse.

Foreign Affairs. 51:380-91. Ja. '73. Western Europe: America's move. B. S. Rosenthal.

Foreign Affairs. 51:573-87. Ap. '73. Rogue elephant in the forest: an appraisal of transatlantic relations. Raymond Vernon.

*Foreign Affairs. 51:747-60. Jl. '73. The Community is working. Theo Sommer.

Foreign Affairs. 52:96-108. O. '73. The concert of Europe. James Chace.

Foreign Affairs. 52:237-48. Ja. '74. The Year of Europe? Z, pseud.

*Foreign Affairs. 52:538-55. Ap. '74. France, the European crisis, and the Alliance. J. O. Goldsborough.

Foreign Affairs. 52:725-41. Jl. '74. Europe and America: a critical phase. Karl Kaiser.

Foreign Policy. 4:62-76. Fall '71. Europe on the move. Walter Scheel.

*Foreign Policy. 12:66-74. Fall '73. Some European questions for Dr. Kissinger. J. R. Schaetzel.

*Fortune. 90:158+. Ag. '74. A bad year for the rich countries. L. A. Mayer.

Guardian (Manchester). p 11. Je. 1, '74. Germany and partners: transfusions and medicines. Michel Boyer.

Guardian (Manchester). p 13. Je. 22, '74. Bonn says no to perpetual surpluses: interview with Chancellor Schmidt. André Fontaine.

International Affairs. 49:1-13. Ja. '73. The European communities act 1972. Geoffrey Howe.

Law and Contemporary Problems. 37:221-7. Spring '72. Perspectives on European unification. Dean Rusk.

Law and Contemporary Problems. 37:228-34. Spring '72. British entry into the Common Market; a British view. B. L. Crowe.

Law and Contemporary Problems. 37:235-46. Spring '72. The United States, the European Community and prospects for a new world economic order. J. M. Leddy.

Law and Contemporary Problems. 37:306-17. Spring '72. The multinational corporation in the enlarged European Community. B. D. Forrow.

Looking Ahead. 22:1. F. '74. A new U.S. hegemony in Western Europe? Theodore Geiger.

Nation. 215:456-63. N. 13, '72. Continental bossism: Common Market, the power trap; membership of Great Britain. R. V. Sampson.

New Republic. 170:15-17. Je. 1, '74. From Pompidou to Giscard d'Estaing. Stanley Hoffmann.

*New York Times. p 41-2. Ja. 14. '73. Testing spirit of Community. C. H. Farnsworth.

*New York Times. p 8. Ag. 15, '73. Discontent with Common Market rising in Britain. Alvin Shuster.

New York Times. p 16. S. 24, '73. The Atlantic gap. Flora Lewis.

New York Times. p 1+. D. 16, '73. Europeans agree on unity in oil crisis. Flora Lewis.

*New York Times. p 8. F. 2, '74. Europe's 9 looking hard at their "crisis." Flora Lewis.

New York Times. p 8. F. 6, '74. Europeans, setting stance for oil talks, rebuff U.S. C. H. Farnsworth.

New York Times. p 28. F. 13, '74. German says Market split cannot be "papered over." C. H. Farnsworth.

*New York Times. p 2. Mr. 11, '74. Strasbourg parliament shows weakness of Europe. Nan Robertson.

New York Times. p 5. Mr. 18, '74. Nixon calls off visit to Europe. David Binder.

New York Times. p 12. My. 1, '74. Political watershed for France. Flora Lewis.

New York Times. p 2. My. 15, '74. A new phase for the Europeans. Flora Lewis.

New York Times. p 9. Je. 6, '74. Britain is warned on Market terms. C. H. Farnsworth.

New York Times. p 5. Je. 11, '74. New bid to Arabs made by Market. C. R. Whitney.

New York Times. p 17. Jl. 14, '74. This is the world that is. C. L. Sulzberger.

New York Times. p 8. O. 19, '74. French suggest closer ties for Europe. C. H. Farnsworth.

New York Times. p 1+. O. 22, '74. Common Market agrees to back joint oil loans. Paul Kemezis.

New York Times. p 3. O. 24, '74. Laborite position shifts, favors Common Market. Alvin Shuster.

New York Times Magazine. p 12-13+. Ja. 20, '74. Idea of Europe runs out of gas. Walter Laqueur.

Newsweek. 79:44. My. 8, '72. Unrousing *oui;* French referendum.

Newsweek. 80:51. O. 9, '72. Norway: stop the world; referendum on Common Market membership.

Newsweek. 82:62+. N. 19, '73. Oil as glue; foreign policy declaration.

Newsweek. 83:50. My. 20, '74. Year Europe lost its head.

Political Quarterly. 44:212-14. Ap. '73. Social policy in the Community.

Round Table. 249:11-21. Ja. '73. The politics of Europe: the power factor. Anthony Hartley.

Round Table. 249:23-38. Ja. '73. The institutions of the Common Market: a British view. J. P. Mackintosh.

Round Table. 249:53-66. Ja. '73. British institutions inside Europe: accepting a new legal order. J. D. B. Mitchell.

*Saturday Review/World. 1:12-15. O. 9, '73. Europe's farm muddle: Common Agricultural Policy of the Common Market. R. C. Longworth.

Science. 184:961-2. My. 31, '74. European Community: pragmatic is the word for the new Europeans.

*Science. 184:962-7. My. 31, '74. In a hard year in Brussels, things look up for science. John Walsh.

*Science. 184:1158-61. Je. 14, '74. European Community energy policy: regulation or mainly information? John Walsh.

*Senior Scholastic. 101:4-13. Ja. 15, '73. European Common Market; symposium.

Time. 99:23-4. Ja. 31, '72. Road to Brussels; ink throwing at British signing ceremony and political hurdles of other governments.

Time. 99:26+. My. 22, '72. Yes to Europe; Irish referendum on Common Market.

Time. 102:37-8. S. 3, '73. Grand disillusion.

Time. 102:42+. D. 17, '73. Toward the summit of truth; Copenhagen summit of Western Europe's heads of government.

Time. 103:49. Je. 10, '74. The Valéry and Helmut show. Bruce Nelan.

U.S. News & World Report. 74:37-9. Ap. 30, '73. What Europe wants from U.S. [interview ed. by Robert Haeger]. Willy Brandt.

U.S. News & World Report. 76:64-6. F. 4, '74. Why the growing rift between U.S. and Europe; symposium.

*U.S. News & World Report. 76:23-4. Ap. 15, '74. U.S. relations with Europe—a shift is in the cards.

U.S. News & World Report. 76:33-4. My. 20, '74. West Europe in disarray—what it means to U.S.

Vital Speeches of the Day. 39:249-51. F. 1, '73. Britain and the Common Market; the revitalization of the European idea; address, November 21, 1972. Roy Jenkins.

Vital Speeches of the Day. 39:269-73. F. 15, '73. Economic relations across the Atlantic; address, November 14, 1972. Giovanni Agnelli.

Vital Speeches of the Day. 39:340-6. Mr. 15, '73. Europe is no scapegoat; address, January 23, 1973. P. M. Boarman.

Vital Speeches of the Day. 40:194-7. Ja. 15, '74. Year of Europe; address, December 13, 1973. J. T. Gurash.

*Vital Speeches of the Day. 40:328-30. Mr. 15, '74. Europe is alive; address, January 29, 1974. Helmut Schmidt.

*Wall Street Journal. p 40. S. 26, '73. Peat, donkeys no longer symbolize Ireland; nation thrives as Common Market member. Bowen Northrup.

*Wall Street Journal. p 1+. D. 17, '73. Common Market delay on oil decision signals slowing of unity drive. R. F. Janssen.

*Wall Street Journal. p 8. Ag. 1, '74. New hope for the Common Market? Robert Prinsky.

*Washington Post. p A 24. F. 6, '74. Common Market disunity. B. D. Nossiter.

World Today. 28:195-201. My. '72. Farm prices and parity in the EEC. Trevor Parfitt.

World Today. 28:424-33. O. '72. Political economics of European monetary integration. Fred Hirsch.

World Today. 29:47-57. F. '73. Foreign policy of the EEC. Ralf Dahrendorf.

World Today. 29:291-9. Jl. '73. America and Europe: a fair bargain in the coming negotiations? John Pinder.

World Today. 29:300-6. Jl. '73. Britain in the European Community: the view from right and left. S. Z. Young.